"Josh Buck offers us an honest, bold, brave, demanding manifesto. His truth-telling is accessible and hard to avoid as he shows the compelling ways in which the gospel becomes a mandate to engage in restorative justice concerning economic matters. His advocacy is deeply based in Scripture and yields practical guidance for good work where God has put us. Buck shows that the gospel cannot be contained in a 'me and Jesus' cocoon but summons us to public issues that concern God's truth for the world. This is an important advocacy that invites us to grow in our awareness and to move our bodies for the sake of the neighborhood."

Walter Brueggemann, Columbia Theological Seminary

"Josh Buck's *Everyday Activism* is exactly what is needed right now to make a difference in the world. He is concise, accurate, insightful, and practical. If you are trying to follow Jesus in real life and real time, this book is a must for the journey!"

Randy Woodley, author, activist, co-sustainer at Eloheh Indigenous Center for Earth Justice and Eloheh Farm & Seeds

"Josh Buck is a trusted friend, a pastor, and an activist-disciple of Jesus Christ. This book promises to be a great introductory guide for thinking about the ethical claim the cross of Christ has for day-to-day life in private and in public. I will be using this in the classroom to help my students learn and practice a just life as faithful disciples and witnesses of Jesus Christ."

Andrew Rillera, PhD, assistant professor of biblical studies and theology at The King's University in Edmonton, AB; coauthor of *Nonviolence*; and author of *Lamb of the Free* (forthcoming, Cascade Books)

"Buck gracefully and honestly shares what it takes to faithfully live as an activist committed to human flourishing and renewal one day at a time. From breaking down terms to practical examples, and with insightful inspiration from the Scriptures, Buck doesn't miss a beat as he proves that activism isn't beyond us but rather is a holy mandate for followers of Jesus. A must-read for everyone committed to embodying the life of Christ."

Tiffany Bluhm, author of *Prey Tell*

"In the introduction to *Everyday Activism*, J.W. Buck writes, 'The truth is that Jesus mobilized ordinary people to do God's work of justice in the world.' This declaration is the heart of *Everyday Activism*. Buck does a beautiful job laying out, in simple terms and with tangible practices, how every single follower of Jesus can be engaged in the work of justice in our everyday lives. Words like *justice* and *activism* are often used but rarely shown how to be applied in the lives of everyday people. Buck does just that. *Everyday Activism* is a must-read for any follower of Jesus wondering how to take the first step in actively engaging the work of justice in our world."

Drew Jackson, pastor, president of Pax, and author of two poetry collections, *God Speaks Through Wombs* and *Touch the Earth*

"Josh Buck's book is for ordinary Christians who suspect that the spiritual and the social are inseparable but who hardly know where to start. This accessible and scripturally based guide from a wise pastor helps overcome the despair of those who think there's nothing they can do and the exhaustion of those who think they must do everything. Buck gently leads the reader toward grace-filled ways of embodying gospel healing in a broken world."

William T. Cavanaugh, DePaul University

"*Everyday Activism* is a rallying cry for white evangelicals to truly practice the radical, peace-filled teachings of Jesus. We need voices who can speak to majority culture believers and say, 'We haven't followed Jesus well. It's time for a new normal.' Josh Buck's *Everyday Activism* is a book every gospel-believing white Christian needs to read."

Michelle Ami Reyes, vice president of the Asian American Christian Collaborative and author of *Becoming All Things*

"Joshua Buck recognizes how a gospel of Jubilee can permeate the personal, cultural, and social dimensions of our world, which informs our daily activism as Christ followers. Grounded in robust narratives tied to Scripture, this book will provide readers with theology, social research, and tactics that can equip Christ-centered activists for ministry in a complex world. Read this book and reclaim a deep conviction that the church can be a restorative partner in a world in need of Jesus's Jubilee."

José Humphreys III, author of *Seeing Jesus in East Harlem* and cofounder of Metro Hope Church in East Harlem, NYC

"*Everyday Activism* makes a case that justice must be at the heart of movement-building. Josh speaks with clear conviction—connecting theology with compelling visuals to bring new insights and perspectives into how we, as Christ followers, can influence our culture toward freedom and flourishing."

Nikole Lim, author of *Liberation Is Here* and founder of Freely in Hope

"*Everyday Activism* offers a renewing gospel vision for both the powerful and the marginalized to follow Jesus. Josh Buck's trauma-informed writing will empower people harmed by distortions of Christian belief and practice to explore a justice-seeking faith that stands against abuses of power. I encourage anyone desiring an insightful and practical guide for discipleship to engage this book!"

Susannah Larry, PhD, assistant professor of biblical studies at Anabaptist Mennonite Biblical Seminary, Elkhart, IN; licensed minister in the Mennonite Church USA; and author of *Leaving Silence*

"Josh Buck offers a much-needed reminder that Christians ought to be activists. *Everyday Activism* reminds readers that Jesus's ministry and day-to-day actions compel us not only to emotionally respond to the brokenness in the world but to consider how we as individuals and collectively as the Church contribute to the brokenness but can also be part of the solution."

Kathy Khang, author of *Raise Your Voice*

"Oftentimes pastors and lay people do not know where to start when beginning an activist journey. J.W. Buck's *Everyday Activism* is an answer to their prayers. Buck masterfully engages issues of power, privilege, and trauma with the gospel message of Jesus. Filled with poignant stories, questions, and takeaways, Buck's book is one that my own white-identifying students can engage as they connect the gospel of Jesus to social justice and activist work. Buck provides an example to follow that will help many others to take their rightful place in activist work. As a Womanist Christian scholar, I appreciate Buck's clear clarion call for white-identifying Christians to engage justice work."

Dr. Angela N. Parker, author of *If God Still Breathes, Why Can't I?*

"*Everyday Activism* is an important resource for the rediscipleship of believers. Beginning with biblical reflections and real-world experiences, Dr. Buck offers a practical tool for Christians searching for ways to recapture a compelling witness for our time. Dr. Buck integrates theological contributions from Latin America and ministry frameworks from leaders in community development to invite readers into a praxis that has sustained the church in the margins for decades. His book will be a necessary tool for congregational leaders and young believers who feel the ministry vision they inherited inadequately responds to the world's social problems."

Emanuel Padilla, president of World Outspoken

Everyday
Activism

Everyday Activism

Following 7 Practices of Jesus
to Create a Just World

J.W. Buck

BakerBooks

a division of Baker Publishing Group
Grand Rapids, Michigan

© 2022 by Joshua Buck

Published by Baker Books
a division of Baker Publishing Group
PO Box 6287, Grand Rapids, MI 49516-6287
www.bakerbooks.com

Printed in the United States of America

Library of Congress Cataloging-in-Publication Data
Names: Buck, J.W. (Joshua W.), author.
Title: Everyday activism : following 7 practices of Jesus to create a just world / J.W. Buck.
Description: Grand Rapids, MI : Baker Books, a division of Baker Publishing Group,
    [2022] | Includes bibliographical references and index.
Identifiers: LCCN 2022014347 | ISBN 9781540902252 (paperback) | ISBN
    9781540902610 (casebound) | ISBN 9781493437788 (ebook)
Subjects: LCSH: Christianity and justice. | Christians—Political activity.
Classification: LCC BR115.J8 B828 2022 | DDC 261.8—dc23/eng/20220524
LC record available at https://lccn.loc.gov/2022014347

Scripture quotations are from the New Revised Standard Version of the Bible, copyright © 1989 National Council of the Churches of Christ in the United States of America. Used by permission. All rights reserved.

Icons and figures were designed by Danny Canales.

The author is represented by the literary agency of Embolden Media Group.

Baker Publishing Group publications use paper produced from sustainable forestry practices and post-consumer waste whenever possible.

22 23 24 25 26 27 28   7 6 5 4 3 2 1

This book is dedicated to King Jesus,
our everlasting foundation for justice,
righteousness, and all that is beautiful in the world.

Contents

Contents

Foreword

It's a strange time to be alive. A global pandemic. Wars and rumors of wars. One church scandal after another. Faith becomes a tenuous thing, especially when there are countless things that we have put our faith in that have failed us . . . people who have failed us. Politicians who have failed us. Pastors and preachers who have failed us.

We are also bombarded with information. The world is at our fingertips. We are blasted with one crisis after another. It becomes impossible to have the energy to respond all the time. And we get compassion-fatigue from trying to care about every injustice that happens day after day.

So, many people give up. They turn it all off and go on with life as usual, or they try to. Others become virtual activists—posting cool sound bites and hot takes on Twitter or creative videos on TikTok, even writing insightful op-eds—but they don't show up in the streets. They have a lot of ideas but can still be mean or aloof. They talk *about* people but not *with* people. They have opinions about issues but are not in relationship with the people directly impacted by those issues. Virtual activism will not solve real-world problems. And virtual community, like virtual food, leaves us very malnourished.

My friend Josh Buck has created a practical resource of daily practices rooted in the life of Jesus that we need to integrate into our lives. How do we live as everyday activists of Jesus? This book helps get us started regardless of what we do for living, how old we are, or if we have formal training.

This book helps us move beyond virtual activism to real activism. It challenges us not just to respond to each new crisis but to integrate activism into our everyday lives. If you find yourself tired and overwhelmed, this book is for you. If you have a hard time knowing how to prioritize issues and injustices and you don't know where to start, this book is for you.

This is a unique book. It is beautiful. It is practical. It is real. It is spiritual. It is part Bible study and part call to action. It is both inward-gazing, looking at the stuff inside ourselves that needs work, and it is outward-gazing, inviting us to live in revolutionary ways.

This book is a gift. Josh Buck is a gift. I trust you will find this project simultaneously practical and inspirational. I pray that what you read leads you into a life that is ready for the next crisis but not waiting around for a crisis. This is a book that invites us to live the revolution every day and to train ourselves so we are ready for whatever the devil throws at us next.

Shane Claiborne, activist, author of *The Irresistible Revolution*, and coauthor of *Jesus for President*

Acknowledgments

There are many layers of people I want to acknowledge. I will limit the list to those who have contributed to my theological and writing journey. Without this cloud of witnesses, I would not have something to say or have written this book. I am incredibly grateful and want to recognize the following people and churches:

My family members who have deeply impacted my writing journey. My incredible wife, Sarswatie Rampersaud Buck, who has shaped my writing since the day we met. My late grandmother Jane Kelley. From the time I was young, Jane would walk me through Scripture late at night before I went to sleep. My parents, Mark and Kathy Buck, who have shown me from a young age what it means to follow Jesus and embrace an active faith in God and commitment to the local church. My brother Jared Smith, who has been a massive joy and writing inspiration. My brother-in-law Braven Greenelsh, who has always been a theological conversation partner. My wonderful sister-in-law Parvati Greenelsh—who has constantly told me I should be writing.

I want to acknowledge my team at Pax, who have given me much faith in the church and in the future of Christianity. This team has helped shape my writing. To Drew Jackson, whose vision, leadership, and poetry will lead us into a brighter tomorrow. Thank you, Mondo Scott, Terry and Julie Diener, Rev. Michael Mata, Genay Jackson, Osheta Moore, and Anna Feingold. To Michelle Ami Reyes, who helped broker the initial meeting with my agent, Jevon. Thanks for offering so much helpful writing advice. And thanks to Dorcas Cheng-Tozun, Missy Pupchik, Kevin Velasquez, Andrew Rillera, Eli Medina, Jai Patel, Travia Forte, and Josue Carballo-Huertas.

To my friends who have been conversation partners for many years, you are a gift beyond measure: Mike Garon, Jarred Clark, Matt Paul, Dillon Nelson, Davis Campbell, Rene and Danny Andalon, David Crammer, Steve Pyfrom, Jeff Henson, Jeff Barich, Edgar Flores, Austin Lack, Josh Lewis, Brian Rayburn, Kris Brossett, Casey Groves, Dan and Kathy Underhill, Emanuel David, Astor Yelangueuzian, Cameron and Ali Mooney, Kevin Bailey, Nolan Hernandez, David Lockwood, Jonathan E. Menéndez, Jeremy Allen, Lamont Hartman, Nikole Lim, Tuan Ngo, Andrew Gates, Andrew Hoffman, James Gann, and Matt Jones. Special thanks to Danny Canales, who did cover and internal design work on this book.

To the various colaborers who helped start Antioch City Church in LA: I arrived at many of my convictions about activism and justice while doing ministry in Highland Park. To Robert, Joanna, Gabby, Alex, and Jayla Cruz: you have been the most wonderful and steadfast ministry partners imaginable. Thanks to Dean and Camila Fletes, Mom and Dad Cruz, Osbert, Ron, Nani Zenay, Aunt Dolly, Uncle Joel, Lance, and Leah. Thanks to Thomas and Dorian Sison, Matt Higby, the Lopez family, Will Quay, David Andrews, David Jee, Blake and Theresa Fisher, Jacob Allen, and Andres and Andrea Pongo. Last but not least, the Andalon clan, through whom I've grown more aware of justice issues within the Mexican-American community.

To the people I sent portions of the book to ahead of time to help shape it: Ernesto Duke, who helped with OT citations and biblical reflections. Emil Haroutunian, who double-checked Scripture references and laid the foundation for the Scripture index. Jon Marshall, who read a few chapters to offer wisdom. Jonathan Nicolai-deKoning, who read through my early manuscript to offer theological suggestions and endnote support. Adam Gustine, who was kind enough to look over my justice matrix to offer suggested improvements.

I want to acknowledge the churches that have impacted my understanding of Jesus, ecclesiology, theology, and activism. Grace Community Church of Auburn, WA; Cornerstone Community Church of Simi Valley, CA; Chapel City Church of Camarillo, CA; Antioch City Church of LA; Fullerton EVFree; Oceanside Christian Fellowship; Anthem Family of Churches; Hope East Village, NYC; Nova Community Church of Torrance, CA; and Southlands Church of Brea, CA.

I'd like to thank many of the mentors, past and present, whom I have learned from and looked up to. Sandra Maria Van Opstal, Dean Mayeda, Jeff Atherstone, Kathy Khang, Shane Claiborne, Gene Poppino, Rev. Michael S. Martin, Mike Edwards, Jarrod Harmaning, Jeff Lilley, Weston Fouche, Jon Marshall, Rev. Anthony Thompson, Rev. Sharon Risher, Dr. John Perkins, Matt Larson, Chuck Bomar, Alejandro Mandes, Steve Highfill, Dan Miller, Geoff Leatherman, Todd Nighswonger, Dan Crane, Allan Barth, and Francis Chan.

I want to honor many of the professors who have shaped my understanding of Jesus. Sameer Yadav, who began rebuilding my imagination of Jesus through historical and cultural analysis. Spencer McCuish, who showed me the power and importance of good questions. Joshua Walker, who modeled humble competence during class. Doug Main, who showed me how to dive deep into the text. My PhD dissertation chair, Dr. Jamie Sanchez, and my committee members Dr. Leanne Dzubinski and Dr. Katrina Greene, who have helped my writing tremendously.

I'd like to thank the team at Baker Publishing Group, who have been incredibly professional, kind, and helpful in this publishing journey. Special thanks to my acquisition editor, Patnacia Goodman, who saw the potential in this book idea before it was fully formed.

I want to acknowledge Jevon Bolden, who founded Embolden Media Group. Thank you for taking me on as a client and believing in my voice as a young writer. The best is yet to come.

Introduction

Main Thought

Jesus calls his followers to engage in the work of justice.

Definitions

Christian activism: Practicing the radical teachings of Jesus to create a just world grew up in a church outside Seattle, Washington, that was planted after a group of people were saved through a Billy Graham crusade. When my family started attending this church in the mid-1990s, it had about three thousand Sunday attendees. We became integrated into this spiritual family pretty quickly:

Sunday services	prayer meetings
youth group	drama performances
choir tours	tithing
Bible studies	membership
mission trips	

You know, the usual. For about eight years, I attended this church until I graduated high school. On the whole, I had a great experience. During those years, the church helped shape my understanding of Jesus, the gospel, and the role I was supposed to play in the world. All my experiences at church were teaching me something about Jesus.

After years of attending church and thousands of hours among this group of Christians, a mental image of Jesus was taking shape. Jesus was a friendly, white, middle-class, well-dressed guy who voted Republican. Jesus preferred verse-by-verse preaching. Jesus was into building projects, high-end kids' programs, midweek Bible studies, and giving 10 percent of your money to sustain a fairly large staff of pastors. Jesus was really into the nuclear family and especially endorsed male leadership. Jesus was suspicious of any spiritual gifts that were considered charismatic. Jesus really wanted you to believe the right things, and the "right things" were always mediated through a reformed Baptist lens. Jesus liked four-part harmonies and orchestras. Jesus liked it when you showed up on time to church.

I learned that Jesus was my private Savior who provided a blueprint for salvation. Jesus wanted us to mature in the faith by sinning less and becoming nicer, more generous people in our private lives. Jesus didn't want me talking too much about money, sex, or politics. Jesus wanted me to develop my "testimony" so I could share how I became a follower of him when prompted.

In all this, Jesus endorsed a quiet, upper-class, and pro-American life.

Despite all the incredible—and not so great—things I learned, I didn't get to know the biblical Jesus very well. The radical Jesus. The activist Jesus. The Jesus from the four Gospels.

Getting to Know the Radical Jesus

Fast-forward to my Bible college years.

I was sitting in a room with fifteen students taking an undergrad class called Life of Christ. In this class, we dedicated ourselves to understanding the historical Jesus. We had to read the four Gospels over and over and read New Testament background books to better understand the historical and cultural context of his day. In this class, I began understanding Jesus within his own context, in his own culture, and on his own terms.

It was incredible. It was surprising. It was jarring.

Don't get me wrong—I also learned some familiar things about Jesus. He was a religious leader who cared about saving people from sin and helping them accept the message of salvation. He cared about our personal piety and our individual responsibility. He also cared that his followers gathered together. Yet, there was so much more I was learning!

During this class, I read stories about Jesus being hunted at birth (Matt. 2:1–15), making crowds mad at the opening of his ministry

(Luke 4:28–30), flipping tables (Matt. 21:12–13), calling religious leaders the walking dead (23:27), purposefully confusing people (Mark 4:10–12), publicly calling out family members (Matt. 12:46–50), running away from mobs trying to arrest him (John 10:39), and ultimately being killed as a Jewish political radical (Matt. 27:37). While Jesus taught his disciples to be peaceful and nonviolent, it was clear he was starting a movement that disrupted the norms of society. I also read about a Messiah who gently pastored people into his movement (John 10:11–18). I learned about a King who did not conform to the social, political, or moral expectations of his day.

Throughout all this, I was asking:

How does this impact my view of justice?
Does this align with the gospel I have accepted?
What does this mean for my everyday life? My church?

I was discovering someone new in the pages of the New Testament.

Then I began studying the various roles of Jesus. He was Rabbi, Son of Man, I AM, King, Lord, Good Shepherd, and Messiah.[1] So many of these titles came loaded with social and political expectations that God would change the world through Jesus.

For Jesus to be the I AM was to place himself in the radical narrative of the exodus, through which God liberated the Israelites both socially and spiritually, politically and religiously.

To be Lord and King was to subvert the false kings in Israel and challenge Caesar.

To be the Son of Man was to bring to remembrance the epic passage Daniel 7:13–14, which tells of how Jesus would disrupt the governments of the world through his own political agenda.

To be the Messiah was to inhabit a Jewish political position that was not welcomed by Rome.

The Gospels showed me that Jesus looked more like a radical activist than a docile, skinny white guy with flowing blond hair who picked up lambs for fun. My conceptions of Christian discipleship were not totally wrong, but they also weren't as biblical as I thought.

While my spiritual heritage is rich, and some of my fondest memories relate to church activity in my youth, there was a massive gap in my Christian imagination. Studying the four Gospels gave me a clear picture of a Jesus who was disruptive, radical, and actively bringing heaven to earth. I saw Jesus teaching us to worship God with a spirit of deliberate activism.

I knew that if I was going to follow this Jesus, I had to adjust to his radical way of life.

Activism for the Rest of Us

While learning about the radical Jesus in the pages of Scripture, I began to feel overwhelmed. I wanted to make a difference in the world, but I wasn't an activist. I worked a lot. I was in school. I wasn't making public speeches on hot-button social issues. Then I became a pastor. During my early years as a pastor, I met with so many people who also wanted to make a difference but didn't feel like they had anything to contribute. They felt like they didn't have enough education, the right personality, or the right life experiences. They felt like they were too broken or didn't have enough time. They were not public speakers, grassroots mobilizers, or people who picketed in front of a business. They considered themselves Jesus followers, but they were ordinary people dealing with their own life struggles.

The reality is that many of us don't have the time, money, connections, or education to be a full-time Christian activist. If you are anything like me, you may find it hard enough to hold your own life together without all the added problems that surround you. And the Bible can sometimes make matters worse. Let me explain.

In the Bible, we read about David fighting a giant (1 Sam. 17), Moses performing miracles in front of Pharaoh (Exod. 7:1–7),

Mary being visited by an angel (Luke 1:26–38), Ruth extending friendship at great personal risk (Ruth 1–4), Ezra heroically leading his people back to Jerusalem (Ezra 8:31–36), and Paul going on a radical journey across the Roman Empire to plant churches (2 Cor. 11:23–26)—not to mention all the people in the hall of faith in Hebrews 11!

What do all these people have in common?

They are all Bible famous.

Yet, when we really look at the numbers, what percentage of people from Bible times are famous? Millions of Israelites were trying to faithfully follow God on an everyday basis, but only a lucky few made a genealogy list. What about the other 99 percent of God's people who were not named as heroes of the faith? These folks were simply looking to follow God in the very average and regular lives they led. They did not make the pages of the Bible for leading revolutions or writing Scripture. No, they simply tried to do the right thing on a daily basis as they negotiated how their faith should impact the various aspects of the world around them. These people were ordinary and normal just like you and me.

The beautiful fact is that the Bible was written to inspire the rest of us to follow God on a mission to love God and people in radical ways. It was written for people who want to make a difference but may not have a spiritual experience propelling them toward full-time Christian ministry.

> If you see the injustice of the world around you and know that Jesus wants you to do something about it—this book is for you.

> If you feel like a regular person living a pleasant yet insular Christian life but you know there's got to be more—this book is for you.

> If you grew up in a church environment that toned down Jesus for the sake of the American dream—this book is for you.

Jesus mobilized ordinary people to do God's work of justice in the world.

> If you read the Gospels and are inspired by the radical Jesus who calls us to bring heaven to the earth around us—this book is for you.
>
> If you don't have the time, capacity, or expertise to become a Christian activist but you know you should be doing more—this book is for you.

The disciples were ordinary people who were trying to get by in a very oppressive and difficult world. The truth is that Jesus mobilized ordinary people to do God's work of justice in the world. In fact, a verse in the Bible illustrates this well. Acts 4:13 says, "Now when they [the masses] saw the boldness of Peter and John and realized that they were uneducated and ordinary men, they were amazed and recognized them as companions of Jesus." This verse was written by Luke after Jesus was unjustly crucified and then resurrected from the grave. By then his followers were going around teaching people about the resurrected Savior. This verse tells us that Peter and John were recognizably undereducated and noticeably normal. Put another way, they were everyday people. But what were they doing? They were being bold and disruptive.

The power God gave to Peter and John is the same power God wants to give to you. The beauty of Christianity is that you don't need to be famous or good-looking. You don't have to be a certain age, height, or weight. You don't need to be highly educated, well-spoken, or born into a particular family. God declares that you have the right to become a child of God (John 1:12) and a coheir with King Jesus (Rom. 8:17) irrespective of those things.

> The New Testament shows us that Jesus specializes in taking those of us who are . . .
>
> normal and making us special
> sinners and actively forgiving us

ordinary and showing us how to be extraordinary
broken and helping us rebuild the world

In this book, I hope to give you a vision for just living by looking at the source—Jesus. In the book *Journey toward Justice*, Nicholas P. Wolterstorff claims that "justice runs like a scarlet thread throughout the New Testament."[2] This book is meant to take that same wonderful scarlet thread of justice from the New Testament and help pull it through our everyday lives.

In chapter 1, I explain how the work of justice connects with the aspects of culture that we interact with on a daily basis. In chapter 2, we will take a look at Jesus's gospel declaration from Luke 4 to root our everyday activism in the gospel of Jubilee. In chapter 3, I explain how social change works, giving practical tools and examples for starting social movements of Jubilee wherever you are at in life. Upon that foundation, in chapters 4 through 10, I unpack seven radical practices of Jesus that show us how to live like everyday activists. Each of these practices is explained through passages from the four Gospels, and they are accompanied by beautiful icons designed by my friend and amazing designer Danny Canales. Seeing these practices demonstrated in Jesus's life, you will be assured that, even amid our busy lives and everyday struggles as Christians, we have been given a divine blueprint of how to share the good news of Jesus in all its magnificent shades of color. The conclusion offers five principles to help you stay in the fight for justice.

The first appendix is called "Justice Matrix," and it will help you process the areas of justice God is calling you to in your everyday life. If you have not thought very much about your local engagement, the second appendix will help you create a plan to get started in justice work. Finally, the third appendix, "Life of Jesus Starter Kit," offers resources if you want to dive deeper into the life of Jesus, historical backgrounds, or theology.

Enough intro'ing. Let's begin!

PART 1

Foundations
for Justice

We are not God. But because we bear God's image, we are worthy of human dignity, love, respect, honor, and protection.

LISA SHARON HARPER

The presence of God is a sanctifying presence: it transforms individuals, communities, societies, and lands.

MUNTHER ISAAC

Chapter One

Creating a Just World

Main Thought

The injustice of the world is caused by sin and manifests in all parts of human culture.

Gospel Connect

The gospel of Jesus propels Christians to defend the dignity of all humans.

Definitions

Imago Dei: Humans reflecting the image of God in the world

Flourishing: Having a right relationship with God, each other, and creation

Justice: Flourishing for everyone

Injustice: Conditions leading to human languishing

Culture: Values, stories, and expressions that humans organize around

Passages to Read

Genesis 1–3; Psalm 89:14; Isaiah 10:1–6

Two years after I finished Bible college, my family and I relocated to northeast Los Angeles to plant a church called Antioch. At this time, Highland Park was primarily a second- and third-generation Mexican American immigrant neighborhood. Amid all its beauty, there was also suffering present, as evidenced by gang activity, violence, poverty, gentrification, and pervasive homelessness. We lived on Piedmont Street right across from the local recreation center and public park.

A year into our church plant, I was working at a local restaurant when I received a phone call from my wife. She sounded uneasy. I quickly asked, "Hey, babe. Everything okay?"

She replied, "I heard gunshots close. It seems like they came from the park."

I replied, "Okay, stay where you are. I'm on my way home now."

While gunshots were normal, it was unusual for my wife to call me about them. I packed my bag and quickly began walking home. As I turned onto Piedmont Street, I saw five police cars, an ambulance, and a bunch of yellow tape around a body lying on the grass across the street from our home. I walked up to our apartment to see if everyone was all right.

After thirty minutes passed, I went to the park to ask the police what had happened. One officer said, "This was a gang-related shooting that started at the high school and ended at this park. It seems like a teenage girl was caught in the gang dispute. Her pursuers chased her here in a car and shot her. Please be careful and stay safe." With sadness, I thanked the officer for the information and went up to tell my family.

Right before sunset, I walked over to the spot of grass where the Latina teenage girl had died of gunshot wounds. I wanted so badly to lead a church that raised up disciples who were peacemakers in a violent city. I was asking God for opportunities to make a difference in this very place. I prayed, "God, will you help me understand the brokenness that exists in this neighborhood? Help me do what Jesus would do. Help me have his ears, eyes, and heart for this area." Looking out over the playground, with children running around and my apartment in the background, I sought wisdom from a God who cares about justice.

One year later, God answered my prayer! Some community leaders asked me to join the recreation center board of advisors. I was excited. We set a plan in motion to put in a drinking fountain next to the playground and mobilize the neighborhood to help find solutions to the homelessness issue. We put pressure on the local city council member to allocate city resources to provide services for under-resourced youth on the block. We worked really hard for about eight months. And guess what the city did with our requests?

Nothing.

That's right.

Nothing.

We had been trying to engage our locally elected officials and get their attention. Then we heard the news that the council member allocated three million dollars to open a brand-new park two miles away from us in a part of Highland Park that was safe and had loads of private investment. I couldn't believe it. I was mad.

Why was this happening?

When we moved to Highland Park, the area was quickly gentrifying. This means that outside investors were buying up property, driving up housing prices, and turning old storefronts into hipster beehives. Families that struggled the most would eventually get kicked out of their dwellings and be forced to find cheaper housing in a different part of the city, and under-resourced churches would be forced to leave storefronts they had been using for years.

The millionaire investors who had moved in to the community were getting the attention of local politicians. As the area was gentrifying and investment was flooding in, the park in front of our apartment was getting worse. The police didn't patrol as much, gang violence was up, and the city refused to properly service the homeless.

So why wasn't the city helping us with the park in front of our apartment? The council member was more interested in cozying up to new homeowners, investors, and political allies in nicer parts of the area. He wasn't as interested in helping to develop the more difficult parts of the neighborhood. In fact, this politician's house was raided a few years later by the FBI on suspicion of corrupt governance.

It angered me to see how the injustice of gentrification was made worse by a crooked local politician. The trickle-down consequences of this evil created social conditions that made it extra hard for local families and youth to have a safe park. I saw how this social injustice put pressure on moms and dads to provide for their kids, and how these conditions were taking a spiritual toll on the young in the area. Our neighborhood council got a few of our items accomplished, but the wheels of justice were not working properly. So I asked myself these questions: How does the gospel apply to these issues of injustice? How can Christians mobilize to change these issues on behalf of Jesus?

Upon reflection, I was convicted about my own role in gentrification. Reading the Old Testament, I saw examples of God holding those with power accountable for not standing up to injustice. I was one of those people who came into the area with more power than most of the Highland Park residents had. For example, when a three-bedroom apartment opened up, the price went from $1,200 a month to $1,900 a month. My tattoo artist told me about it, and my four-person family took the apartment. This meant that we were a part of the economic problem causing many families to suffer in the face of a changing community. While thousands of Christians in Highland Park were praying for a way to pay the new rent prices, I was taking part in driving up those prices! What does Jesus teach us about this? What does justice look like in this situation? Through this event, I learned about how sinfulness and evil work their way into a culture, social structures, and systems.

When did you realize that injustice is a normal part of life? Was there a moment in your life when you had a similar realization that God cares about what is happening in the world? The great thing about the Bible is that it gives us language to identify injustices around us and provides a blueprint for cultural renewal. Through the examples we find in God's Word, we see that God cares about injustice and wants his followers to bring justice into their present situations.

The aim of this chapter is to show that from the beginning of God's story, we see a focus on justice. While we all know the world is broken, we need a common story and a common language in order to see clearly what Jesus teaches us about how we, as ordinary Christians, can pursue justice in our everyday lives. God cares about the injustices that surround us.

Common Language and Sacred Story

It all starts in the beginning.

In the book of Genesis, we read about a powerful, creative, and peaceful God creating everything to be good. All was good!

The pattern goes something like this:

God spoke → Creation burst forth → It was good

The actions of God in creation were inherently good because God is good. Everything God did and said was just. It was right. It was well. On this point, the psalmist declares, "Righteousness and justice are the foundation of your throne; steadfast love and faithfulness go before you" (Ps. 89:14). It was from God's divine throne of justice, righteousness, love, and faithfulness that everything was created.[1] This means that the world is a reflection of God's just character, which leads us to my definition of justice: flourishing for everyone. From the character of God flows justice. We see in Genesis that from God's throne of justice everything was created to flourish. When flourishing happens, everyone is in right relationship with their Creator God, each other, and creation itself.

The Imago Dei

On the sixth day of creation, God created humans, both men and women, in his image and likeness (Gen. 1:26–28). *Imago Dei* is a Latin phrase that means humans reflecting the image of God in the world.[2] Scripture says, "So God created humankind in his image, in the image of God he created them; male and female he created them" (Gen. 1:27).

The image of God in all humans, or the imago Dei, is central to establishing the purpose for Christian activism. There are three things we need to know about being made in God's image. First, we have been given immeasurable dignity and worth as humans. Second, we share certain character traits with God. Third, we are called to embody the imago Dei by creating good things in the world.

Intrinsic Dignity and Worth

First, the imago Dei means that all humans are to be treated with dignity and respect. To be made in the image of God is to have immeasurable and eternal worth. This means that it is impossible to put a price on a human. All humans—regardless of social status, nationality, lineage, IQ, wrongdoing, gifting, sexuality, or cultural background—have a worth that is irrevocable. This means that all of us have the right to flourish among each other. And for humans to flourish, we must be in a right relationship with God, each other, and creation. African American theologian Vincent E. Bacote writes, "The biblical view of humans as divine image bearers establishes our identity as the unique pinnacle of God's creation order and as those whose common status serves as a basis for mutual respect."[3]

We know this to be true because God put a number of provisions in the Hebrew law that affirmed human dignity and worth. God instituted gleaning laws so under-resourced people and immigrants could work and survive (Lev. 19:9–10). God created the Sabbath, in part, so that humans were not overworked by unjust rulers or employers (Deut. 5:12–14). God allowed people to offer alternative, less-expensive animals for sacrifice if they were struggling financially (Lev. 14:30). God created cities of refuge so that accused parties could get a fair trial (Josh. 20). These are just some of many examples in the Old Testament that reveal the dignity and worth granted to those created in the image of God. God's people were to express obedience and worship by protecting everyone who bore God's image. We also see the value God puts on human life in how Jesus came to die in order to dignify all of us through the offer of salvation. Through the cross, God offers every human the opportunity to receive divine protection, forgiveness of sins, and eternal life.

These examples reveal the worth that all humans have been given. In fact, the biblical teaching on the imago Dei is the Christian foundation for all human rights.[4] The implications of this truth are massive, and they are seen in how Jesus loved people, served people, and died on the cross to give image bearers a chance to restore their relationship with God.

Sharing Character Traits

Second, to be made in the image and likeness of God means that we share certain character traits with God. In this way, God put a divine mark on all humans.

We, like God, . . .

> are creative
> are emotive

are logical

share stories

have purpose

find meaning

desire community

create family

desire justice

The divine fingerprint of God has been placed on each and every human across all time and space. While animals share some of the qualities mentioned above, the combination and scale of the attributes God has given humans make us different. The way we long for meaning. The way we desire to have purpose. The way we wrestle with our conscience. The way we long for justice when someone wrongs us! Eloise Meneses notes that those made in God's image "are to care for the created order through the construction of peaceful communities."[5] God created a peaceful and just garden. He created humans made in his image to create a peaceful and just world. And to be made in the image of a just God is to long for and enact justice in the world. So how do we reflect God's just character in the world? The next section will show us.

Cocreators

Third, humans are meant to reflect God in the world by creating good things. In Genesis 1:28–31, God tells Adam and Eve to go into the world, take care of creation, create a family, and take care of the animals.[6] Put simply, God wants humans to go into the world to do good things and create good things.[7] Because a good world is full of peace and justice, this means that God created humans in his image to do justice, be just, and promote justice in the world. When we do these things, we are promoting the very nature of God in the world. Before sin was introduced into creation, it was natural for humans to flourish. Justice was natural. Justice was normal. Justice was living in a right relationship with God, each other, and creation. God created humans to treat each other with spiritual, emotional, psychological, physical, and cultural dignity. What does this look like?

When humans cultivate the world in justice . . .

> People protect each other.
> Everyone has enough to eat.
> Judges make the right decisions.
> Rights are extended to everyone.
> Mutual respect is a common value.
> Humans worship God above all.
> Punishment leads to restoration.
> Power is used for the uplifting of others.
> The imago Dei is valued in everyone.

When we carry out God's mandate to help the world flourish, we end up promoting justice in the world.[8] Humans become cocreators with a just God by following the call of Micah 6:8, where God says to his people, "What does the LORD require of you but to do justice, and to love kindness, and to walk humbly with your God?" This verse is key to our duty as everyday activists. In *God Loves Justice*, Jessica Nicholas writes, "Doing 'justice and righteousness' means loving the things that lead to life and actively righting the wrongs that keep people from experiencing life as God created it to be."[9] We bear God's image in the world by calling people to a right relationship with God, each other, and creation. In the process of doing this, humans manifest the justice and righteousness of God in the world.

To recap our common story: God created everything good, including humans. God created humans in his image. Being created in the image of God means that we (1) have immeasurable dignity and worth, (2) share the attribute of justice with God, and (3) are to cocreate good things in the world alongside God. Michael W.

God created humans
in his image to do justice,
be just, and promote
justice in the world.

Goheen and Craig G. Bartholomew note, "To be human means to have huge freedom and responsibility, to respond to God and to be held accountable for that response."[10] This freedom and responsibility manifest in our call to go and be just in the world. When this happens, we live our imago Dei call to be in relationship with God, see others treated justly, and see creation flourish. So what went wrong?

Sin Leading to Injustice

In Genesis 3, Adam and Eve eat fruit from a tree that God forbade them to eat from. Adam and Eve do something that is not good. When humans do something outside their design, the Bible calls this sin, unrighteousness, or evil. When Adam and Eve ate the fruit, they engaged in disobedience and evil before God. It was immoral and wrong and led them away from the flourishing they had experienced until then. With that one decision, Adam and Eve rejected their calling as bearers of God's image.

Figure 1.1 illustrates the two trajectories all of us find ourselves on in the world. Our decision to reflect or reject God's image sets us on a trajectory toward either flourishing or languishing. Every human has the choice to reject or embrace the duties inherent to bearing the image of God in the world. When we reflect God properly, we help create a more just world where all can flourish. When we reject the image of God within, we create unjust conditions all around us. If justice is reflecting God's image so all can flourish, then injustice is creating conditions that lead to languishing.

FIGURE 1.1

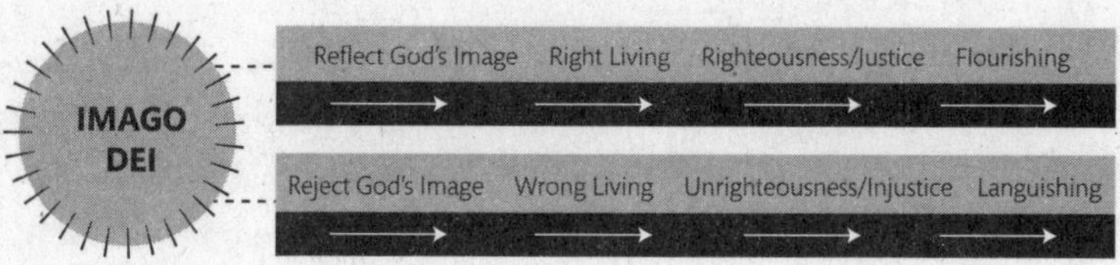

IMAGO DEI

| Reflect God's Image | Right Living | Righteousness/Justice | Flourishing |

| Reject God's Image | Wrong Living | Unrighteousness/Injustice | Languishing |

When we live and create outside our design, we create a scarcity of resources; we see abuses of power; we take part in cultural subjugation, ethnocentrism, violent relationships, fearful workplaces, and economic imbalances. And we create conditions in which humans do not have access to the knowledge of Jesus. We treat some people as more sacred or better than others. Injustice is present when the imago Dei is not valued equally among people. When this happens, God uses those made in his image to take up the cause of justice in the world.

What does this tangibly look like? A passage from the book of Job illustrates God's heart and desire to see this world restored. It is possible for all humans to flourish only when God's people actively pursue justice in their everyday lives. In the passage below, Job is in the middle of his defense before God. Job appeals to the ways in which he reflected God's image by pursuing justice and by supporting fellow humans who were suffering unjust treatment.

> I delivered the poor who cried,
>> and the orphan who had no helper.
> The blessing of the wretched came upon me,
>> and I caused the widow's heart to sing for joy.
> I put on righteousness, and it clothed me;
>> my justice was like a robe and a turban.
> I was eyes to the blind,
>> and feet to the lame.
> I was a father to the needy,
>> and I championed the cause of the stranger.
> I broke the fangs of the unrighteous,
>> and made them drop their prey from their teeth.
>> (Job 29:12–17)

In these verses, Job claims that he was righteous and holy before God because he lived justly before the most marginalized and vulnerable around him. If you were going to make an appeal to God, would you be able to defend yourself like Job did in these verses?

Now that we have assumed a common story and defined terms, let's see how justice and injustice work their way out in our society and the cultural systems around us.[11]

Defining Culture

Culture can be defined very simply as values, stories, and expressions that humans organize around.[12] There are roughly seven aspects of culture that humans are constantly creating and organizing around: government/politics, economics, work, customs/traditions, family, arts, and language (see fig. 1.2). These aspects of culture can also be called cultural systems.[13] Every human reflects God in the world when they engage in these aspects of culture.[14]

FIGURE 1.2

Seven Aspects of Culture

Government/ Politics Economics Work Customs/ Traditions

Family Arts Language

Human Values + Stories + Expressions

IMAGO DEI

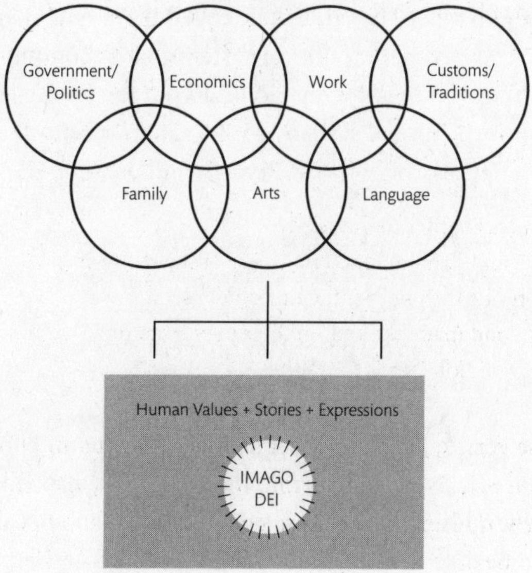

The seven aspects of culture are meant to be created and sustained by humans with the goodness and justice of God. When this happens, all humans flourish in the world. God made humans to create good governments, good economics, good work environments, good customs, good families, good art, and good languages. If created properly, each of these seven cultural sectors is equitable, is full of love and hope, and promotes the rights of everyone without bias. What does this look like? Every human has access to a saving knowledge of King Jesus. Every human has a family system that is supportive, a community without violence, clean water, enough food, medical rights, economic mobility, benevolent leaders, and the ability to grow into the person God designed them to be. He desires that every person exist within their cultural setting without sin being committed against them. God also expects each individual to do the hard internal work so they display the fruit of the Spirit (Gal. 5:22–23) and practice justice properly in these aspects of culture. We worship God by creating and cultivating good culture around us.

In the Old Testament, God called his people to create just systems of culture, and when they didn't, he called them out. Consider the creation of government, political systems, and economic policies in Israel. In the book of Isaiah, God calls out the Jewish leaders for not creating just cultural systems.[15] Who suffers the most from these unjust and oppressive policies? Read to find out.

> Ah, you who make iniquitous decrees,
>   who write oppressive statutes,
> to turn aside the needy from justice
>   and to rob the poor of my people of their right,
> that widows may be your spoil,
>   and that you may make the orphans your prey!
> What will you do on the day of punishment,
>   in the calamity that will come from far away?
> To whom will you flee for help,
>   and where will you leave your wealth,

> so as not to crouch among the prisoners
>> or fall among the slain?
> For all this his anger has not turned away;
>> his hand is stretched out still. (Isa. 10:1–4)

These verses are a sobering reminder that God desires his followers to reflect true justice and mercy as we image God in the world. He demands justice because every single human has been made in God's image. God gave widows as much humanity as politicians, and vulnerable immigrants as much worth as the rich. When the scales of justice get out of balance, God desires for us to help restore justice in the world. Christians have been given the epic responsibility of stewarding and caring for these aspects of culture and making sure that those who follow Jesus are carefully, persistently, and actively moving these cultural systems in a more just direction.

Is this easy?

Not at all! For most of us, it is difficult to imagine making major changes in culture. Often we feel that the seven aspects of culture are too broken for us to make a difference. Perhaps you want something to change, but you are discouraged because the problem is too big or complex. Take heart! Brazilian theologian Ivone Gebara talks about how the everyday activism of ordinary Christians can make a difference when they come together to stand up to those in power. She writes, "These ordinary actions, enlarged to collective dimensions, will perhaps become dangerous for those who hold power over others. These ordinary acts call into question societies incapable of taking into consideration the common good over individual selfishness."[16] This is the work of the everyday activist. Whether in a position of authority or working hard under broken cultural systems, we value the imago Dei in every human as we fight to create just culture around us. Our spiritually rooted, ordinary actions can change the world. We can make a difference together, one holy act of resistance at a time. In the next chapter, we explore the gospel of Jubilee as the foundation on which we become everyday activists.

Everyday Activist
T A K E A W A Y S

1 *Everyday activists recognize that the spiritual and the social are inseparable and have a massive impact on each other.*

Genesis 1 teaches us that the physical world and the spiritual world are connected and impact each other in many ways. When considering everyday activism, we cannot address the physical need without addressing the spiritual need any more than we can address the spiritual need without addressing the social needs of people. Both are critical when we consider how we can promote human flourishing and the protection of those made in the image of God.

2 *Everyday activists identify the cultural evils and unjust systems that they are a part of.*

Think about the seven aspects of culture identified in this chapter. Whether we like it or not, we take part in various aspects of culture that dehumanize others. This cannot be avoided. It is essential to discern how we can be caught in a culture that does not treat people well. Does your family system treat some better than others? What forms of violence surround you that are easy to ignore? The biggest enemy of justice is those who refuse to acknowledge their part in an unjust system.

3 *Everyday activists consider how the truths about the imago Dei have the capacity to impact their everyday lives.*

We learned in this chapter that humans have been given immeasurable worth, that we share certain character traits with God, and that we are called to embody the imago Dei by creating good things in the world. How can these truths shape your everyday life? How do these truths shape the way you engage in the seven aspects of culture? Do these truths change the way you view your own body, mind, and desires? How can you promote human flourishing through the role God gave you in the world?

Foundations for Justice

Reflection Questions

How does God's heart for justice and human flourishing impact your outlook on life?

What groups of people are robbed of the dignity afforded them by the imago Dei?

Who can you join hands with on a daily basis to defend fellow humans made in the image of God?

Which of the seven aspects of culture do you find yourself engaging in on a regular basis? How can you have an influence for human flourishing in those areas?

Jesus is the daily and eternal fulfillment to the Year of Jubilee. Justice and equality, provision and freedom, salvation and healing of all creation are found in Christ.

RANDY S. WOODLEY

Jubilee is a rich idea woven through the storyline of the Bible. Yet we don't hear many Christians talking about it today.

KIM TAN

Chapter Two

The Gospel of Jubilee

Main Thought

The first step of everyday activism is to embrace the gospel of Jubilee.

Gospel Connect

The gospel's power to save is the same power to create a just world.

Definitions

Jubilee: Spiritual life and social flourishing

Holistic gospel: The good news for all creation

Disjointed gospel: Separating spiritual life and social flourishing

Passages to Read

Luke 4:16–21; Isaiah 61:1–11; Leviticus 25:8–55

L et me ask you a question: What is the gospel? Sit and think about this for a minute. If you were to sum up the gospel in one sentence, what would it be? I grew up learning that Jesus died on the cross to save me from my sins so I can live a new life. New life had to do with sinning less, attending church, being a peaceful person, and awaiting heaven. The gospel was largely understood through biblical terms like *born again* and *justification*. Despite all the great things I learned in church, the gospel I was taught did not connect very well to the issue of justice, nor did it incorporate Jesus's own teachings from the Gospels.[1] When I opened up the four Gospels to let Jesus shape my understanding of the Good News, I began seeing God's vision to bring heaven to earth (Matt. 6:10) in tangible ways that affect culture in the world. When Jesus became my starting point, everything changed.

Jesus must be our starting point when looking to define, understand, and explain the gospel. What is the gospel? Start with Jesus. Who is the gospel for? Start with Jesus. How does the gospel connect to justice? Start with Jesus. In what way does the gospel fit into the Jewish narrative of Scripture? Start with Jesus. How does Jesus's teaching on the gospel connect with other explanations from other biblical writers?

IT STARTS WITH JESUS.

If we are going to start with Jesus, we must go to the opening moments of Jesus's ministry, where he teaches us about the gospel. Argentinian theologian Esteban Voth calls Jesus's gospel declaration in Luke 4:16–21 "the Great Omission" because we so often skip over it.[2] Jesus must be our starting point to understand the gospel as

Jesus must be our starting
point when looking
to define, understand,
and explain the gospel.

everyday activists, so let's head into this passage in order to create a firm foundation for the work of justice and mercy.[3]

The Gospel of Jubilee

In Luke 4, we see the opening moments of Jesus's public ministry. Jesus is in the synagogue of his small hometown and offers an interpretation of a passage that he reads in public. Jesus is in a social setting where people know him. He is among friends, family, and those he grew up with. In this passage, Jesus teaches us to embrace the gospel of Jubilee.[4]

Luke writes:

> When he [Jesus] came to Nazareth, where he had been brought up, he went to the synagogue on the sabbath day, as was his custom. He stood up to read, and the scroll of the prophet Isaiah was given to him. (Luke 4:16–17)

Jesus is handed a scroll from Isaiah 61. Before we read further in Luke 4, we need to know a few things. First, Isaiah 61 was a very familiar text for the Jewish crowd listening to Jesus. It is a passage about God delivering the Jews from a terrible situation and punishing their enemies. Second, Isaiah 61 connects directly back to Leviticus 25, where God created an amazing Jewish institution called the Year of Jubilee.[5] What does the Year of Jubilee mean exactly? Every fifty years, God restored justice. God's people were to release the enslaved (25:39), avoid predatory lending (25:13–17), let the land rest (25:11), and reset real-estate prices (25:23). Jubilee meant that those who had suffered from generational debt to others were able to start over. In this year, the land and everyone in Jewish society could rest. While this meant that the wealthy and well-to-do citizens had much to lose, it also meant that the poor and oppressed experienced God's Jubilee. For the rich, God challenged their accumulation of wealth and called them to live like Jesus (Mark 10:17–22).

The Year of Jubilee signaled God's grace toward those who were oppressed and his check on those who had leverage over the poor. One scholar summarizes Jubilee as universal hospitality, lavish abundance, and social solidarity toward those in need.[6] It was God's justice, mercy, and grace being activated in a very tangible way on earth. Why would God do this? Those who are poor and oppressed in any society end up being robbed of the human dignity afforded them by the imago Dei. Their rights are canceled. Their collectors abuse them. Their masters become violent. Their religious leaders dismiss them. The economy presses them down. God is not okay with this. God created the Year of Jubilee to balance the scales of justice among his people.

Now that we have some context for the passage Jesus is reading, let's get back to Luke 4.

> He unrolled the scroll and found the place where it was written:
>
> > "The Spirit of the Lord is upon me,
> >   because he has anointed me
> >   to bring good news to the poor.
> > He has sent me to proclaim release to the captives
> >   and recovery of sight to the blind,
> >   to let the oppressed go free,
> > to proclaim the year of the Lord's favor."
>
> And he rolled up the scroll, gave it back to the attendant, and sat down. The eyes of all in the synagogue were fixed on him. Then he began to say to them, "Today this scripture has been fulfilled in your hearing." (vv. 17–21)

Jesus claims that he is anointed by God to bring good news to those who are poor. Jesus says that he came to declare release for the prisoners and sight for the blind and to let those oppressed go free. He is to proclaim the year of the Lord's favor. Then, if this announcement isn't provocative enough, Jesus claims that Isaiah 61 is being fulfilled on the very day he is reading it!

This is not ordinary.

This is not keeping the peace.

This is radical.

Jesus's words were not normal for a rabbi but the words of a King who has a right to rule over the world and institute justice for those who suffer. Those who grew up with Jesus didn't like what he was saying. Jesus said that the gospel, or "Good News," will reach the disenfranchised, the outcast, the sinner, the prisoner, those who are blind, and the oppressed. How did his friends, neighbors, and family respond to his teaching on the gospel of Jubilee? They tried to kill him. We learn from this that those who follow Jesus into his radical teachings on Jubilee will often be rejected by the people they are closest to.

In Luke 4, Jesus tethers his gospel to the historically rich Jewish concept of Jubilee from Leviticus 25.

Two things help us understand the gospel of Jubilee as a foundation for everyday activism. First, the gospel of Jubilee declares that we can receive spiritual life. Second, the gospel of Jubilee declares that everyone should have access to social flourishing. These two facets of Jubilee form a biblically rooted holistic gospel that is the foundation for works of justice and mercy in the world. We will see that the gospel of Jubilee speaks to four areas: spiritual, social, individual, and collective.

Jubilee Means Spiritual Life for Individuals

The gospel of Jubilee calls people to spiritual life. Humans have been offered spiritual redemption through the blood sacrifice of Jesus (Eph. 1:7; Heb. 10:1–18). When we place our faith in the work of Jesus on the cross, we receive the free gift of spiritual life (Eph. 2:8–9). Whether you are rich or poor, oppressed or oppressor, Jew or Gentile, you can inherit eternal life if you acknowledge you need Jesus to save you from your sin (Mark 2:10). To obtain spiritual life, you must admit that you are not king, that you have sinned and lived outside God's design, and that a King named Jesus stands over your life (Phil. 2:10–11). Once you receive this salvation, you are adopted into the family of God (John 1:12–13) and receive the gift of the Holy Spirit (John 15:26). In addition, Ecuadorian theologian C. René Padilla teaches us that "salvation includes a complete restoration of man and woman as the image of God."[7] Did you catch that? God restores our humanity through the salvation offered in Christ! Our spiritual life in Christ sets us free to reflect God properly in the world. Spiritual Jubilee is offered through the sacrifice Jesus made on the cross.

Zechariah speaks about the deep spiritual need that Israel was longing for and how his son would prepare the way for Jesus: "And you, child, will be called the prophet of the Most High; for you will go before the Lord to prepare his ways, to give knowledge of salvation to his people by the forgiveness of their sins" (Luke 1:76–77). Jesus came to tell people that salvation comes through the forgiveness of sins. The call of Jesus to spiritual life guards against those longing for societal justice without personal transformation. The gospel of Jubilee teaches us that our responsibility before God to repent and accept the sacrifice of Jesus is central to becoming an everyday activist.

Jubilee Means Social Flourishing for All

While the gospel is about salvation and the restoration of humans as individuals, it is also about the restoration of the entire cosmos to God (Col. 1:19–20). This means that the gospel explained in Luke 4:16–21 can't be applied just to individuals and can't speak only to our spiritual life. The gospel offers not only spiritual Jubilee for individuals but also social Jubilee for the collective. As Filipina theologian Melba Padilla Maggay says, "When we say 'Jesus is Lord,' it is not just a confession, it is a cosmic and social fact."[8]

The gospel of Jubilee calls us to seek the flourishing of everyone around us. How do we know this? Jesus sets his good news within the biblical passages of Leviticus 25 and Isaiah 61, which means that the gospel is attached to the Old Testament story and the context of these two passages. Leviticus 25 is about protecting those on the margins of society, offering help to those who need it, subverting the social systems that lead to oppression, and giving scandalous grace to those who seemingly don't deserve it. It is all about justice! The Year of Jubilee was about restoring the dignity and humanity of everyone in Israel. Jubilee was also about showing all the other nations that the one true God was Yahweh. If Israel practiced Jubilee, the rest of the world would witness that Yahweh was benevolent, was compassionate, and cared about those who languished under injustice. If Jubilee was enacted, the gods of other nations would be put to shame and the one true God of Israel would be glorified. Yet, we have no evidence that Israel ever practiced God's Jubilee![9] Why? While it is difficult to say, I am willing to assume that Jubilee was impractical, too radical, and disturbed too many wealthy Jewish land and slave owners. Yet, Jubilee was the call of Israel and is the call of everyone who calls upon Jesus for salvation. Jubilee is the gospel call of the church in this very generation.

Even though Jesus had to run away from a hometown mob after reading at the synagogue, Luke shows us the outworking of the gospel of Jubilee throughout the rest of his book. Jesus opens his ministry with the gospel of Jubilee, preaches the gospel of Jubilee, and lives out the gospel of Jubilee. In the Gospel of Luke, Jesus offers physical healing (7:21). He teaches his followers to give to everyone who asks without demanding repayment (6:30, 35), to share possessions (3:11), and to be merciful and forgive others (6:36–38). Jesus is clear that he came to save the poor and oppressed (4:18–19), pronounce woes against the rich (6:24–25), and confront the Pharisees, whom he calls "lovers of money" (16:14). Jesus tells his followers to invite the poor, lame, and blind to dinner because God has invited the same people to the banquet table of salvation (14:12–14). Jesus radically includes and protects those on the margins and routinely confronts the leaders who take part in cultural systems that are unjust. In all these verses, we can hear echoes of Isaiah 61 and Leviticus 25.

The gospel of Jubilee is our radical starting point for how we are to be disciples of Jesus in the world. It is clear that "Luke presents Isaiah as foundational for how Jesus viewed his ministry—an example followed by his disciples."[10] This example must be proclaimed and embodied in the world. We must allow the gospel of Jubilee to frame our understanding of Christian service in the world. The social and collective call of the gospel of Jubilee does not allow Christians to disconnect personal salvation from the care for justice in the world.

The Holistic Gospel of Jubilee

In the Western world, we have incorrectly divided the gospel into four separate areas: spiritual, social, individual, and collective.[11] Some Christians emphasize the gospel's spiritual call to personal transformation and individual responsibility. These folks often emphasize individual piety as the highest expression of faith in Jesus. This group calls us to evangelize so souls are saved. Other Christians emphasize social responsibility toward our neighbors in need. These folks often elevate social activism as a manifestation of Christlikeness. Some cultures emphasize the collective call to live justly, while many people in the West emphasize individual just living over corporate responsibility.

You confused yet?!

If you have learned about the gospel in the Western world, consider how you may have learned to divide the gospel into these four categories. As the chart shows, such division leads to a disjointed gospel. Fortunately, the gospel of Jubilee accounts for all four areas.

Disjointed Gospel	
Spiritual	**Social**
Regeneration	Transformation
Piety	Renewal
Righteousness	Justice
Individual	**Collective**
Personal belief	Public good
Personal message	Corporate responsibility
Personal growth	Equitable resources

FIGURE 2.1

Holistic Gospel

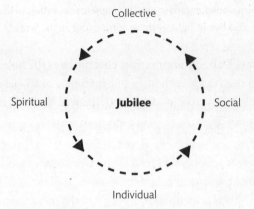

Here is the truth: Jesus did not honor these divisions when he declared and lived out the gospel of Jubilee! The separations are false dichotomies that have been developed throughout church history and within the Western church and that are a massive distraction from the biblical concept of Jubilee. The gospel is fully spiritual, fully physical, fully individual, fully collective, fully about individual transformation, and fully about social transformation.[12] The writers of the New Testament do not honor these distinctions that divide the social from the spiritual. Instead, the gospel of Jubilee is a vision for holistic world transformation (see fig. 2.1).[13]

Let me end with the question I posed at the beginning of this chapter: What is the gospel? Jesus answered the question when he declared a holistic gospel of Jubilee that addresses our spiritual nature and the social evils that surround us.[14] It is upon this foundation that we can pursue justice in the world.

I will leave you with the reflections of Latin American theologian Ruth Padilla DeBorst, who beautifully communicates what it means to accept the gospel of Jubilee and spread it in the world:

Belonging, in God's new humanity, is a condition freely granted to all who admit to their created condition, acknowledge Jesus Christ as Savior and Lord, recognize that their very breath depends on the living Spirit, look forward to God's complete restoration of the entire creation, and live in light of these confessions in the world.[15]

The gospel DeBorst summarizes encompasses the holistic restoration God desires for each of us to experience in Christ—it is the restoration God is calling us to participate in that will allow our world to flourish.

Everyday Activist
TAKEAWAYS

1 *Everyday activists embrace the gospel as holistic transformation.*

African American activist and theologian Barbara A. Holmes writes, "The quest for justice begins with participation in the claim that we are redeemed by a suffering Savior."[16] Our quest starts with our own redemption and begins to play out in larger ways in society. Does your understanding of the gospel account for holistic world transformation? How does the gospel of Jubilee impact your own life? Have you accepted the gospel of Jubilee? What are the cultural and social impacts of this gospel on the world around you?

2 *Everyday activists place themselves within the biblical narrative.*

In Luke 4, Jesus begins his public ministry by placing himself within the biblical narrative. Jesus connects himself to the land, the people, his ethnic heritage, and the nations that need him. Jesus calls us into a Jewish faith story that creates boldness and action in our lives. We have a new story. We have a new leader. We were adopted into the story of God to become everyday activists!

3 *Everyday activists are called to fight for the social and spiritual Jubilee of those who are oppressed.*

In Luke 4, Jesus reads a part of the biblical story that points toward radical social and spiritual change in order to explain the gospel. Christians are bound to these verses and this story. Who are the people around you who need this Jubilee? Who needs to know the freedom God is offering them in Christ? What social structures keep people from experiencing Jubilee? These questions are foundational in the fight for justice in the world.

Foundations for Justice

Reflection Questions

How does Luke 4 impact your view of the Christian life?

How does the concept of Jubilee impact your understanding of the gospel?

What would it look like to live out the holistic gospel of Jubilee in your everyday life?

Each new hour holds new chances. . . .
Offering you space to place
new steps of change.

MAYA ANGELOU

Small groups of regular individuals—
that is, with the same amount of social
power and resources as everyone else—
can successfully initiate a change in social
conventions. The power of small groups
comes not from their authority or wealth
but from their commitment to the cause.

ANDREA BARONCHELLI et al.

Chapter Three

How Social Change Happens

Main Thought

Jubilee is possible when Christians mobilize together.

Gospel Connect

The gospel of Jubilee that changes our lives is meant to be carried into the world to create change.

Definitions

Gospel power: The power that comes when we proclaim and embody the gospel message

Momentum point: The point at which enough people have social buy-in to create cultural momentum

Critical mass: The percentage of people in a cultural system who need to be in favor of a change for the culture to change

Passages to Read

Romans 1:16; 1 Peter 3:15; Matthew 5:13–16

The first two chapters set a foundation for why we are supposed to seek justice in the world. This third foundational chapter answers another very important question: Is it really possible to change the world as an ordinary person? After all, this book is written for people with full schedules and long work hours and for those who don't consider themselves educated or gifted enough to be an activist.

Is it really possible for ordinary followers of Jesus to create a just world?

You might not be picketing in the streets, writing an op-ed for the *New York Times*, speaking at a rally, or pursing a degree lending itself to activism, and that is okay. Neither did the disciples of Jesus! But they were still able to bring about radical social change. In this chapter, we are going to focus on how you, in your everyday life, can become the change right where you are. First, I will show how the gospel itself is powerful enough to change the world. This mysterious spiritual truth will undergird everything we do. Second, we will look at the theory of social change to explore how we can usher in Jubilee right where God has placed us.

The Power of the Gospel

Before we look at the latest research on how to create social change, we must first understand a truth that resides deep within the foundations of the universe: the greatest power we possess to change the world is in the declaration and embodiment of the gospel.

The power of the gospel is active.

The power of the gospel is overwhelming.

The power of the gospel is mysterious.

The power of the gospel flows through us.

The same power that gave life to the crucified body of Christ flows through each and every human who embraces the gospel of Jubilee.

Jubilee Proclaimed

First, followers of Jesus tap into the power of God when they proclaim the gospel of Jubilee. Paul wrote to the church in Rome, "For I am not ashamed of the gospel; it is the power of God for salvation to everyone who has faith, to the Jew first and also to the Greek" (Rom. 1:16). This verse is really important! Paul is teaching us that God's power is activated when we share about Jesus. This does not mean we need to become an evangelist or share our faith every moment of every day. It does mean that we should be willing to let people know why we care about justice and mercy. We should always be ready to give an answer to the "why" when we are asked about our activism (1 Pet. 3:15). When we declare Jubilee, like Jesus did in Luke 4, wonderful things happen around us. People get saved. People get healed. People receive the Holy Spirit. People join a movement. God is always at work through the message of the gospel. While some find the gospel of Jubilee foolish and others find it offensive (1 Cor 1:22–25), we can't back down from sharing about Jesus, who died to set us free from the shame and sin that shackle us. Moreover, as Christians, we must believe and abide in this message of Jubilee ourselves. Bethany Hanke Hoang and Kristen Deede Johnson write, "Those of us who desire to seek justice also need to experience the freedom and transformation that comes in and through Jesus Christ."[1] We must first receive this message on a daily basis. But then we must be willing to share it with others.

Jubilee Embodied

Second, everyday activists tap into the power of God when they embody the gospel of Jubilee. While some people will respond to

The greatest power
we possess to change the
world is in the declaration
and embodiment
of the gospel.

the power of the proclaimed gospel, others will come to faith in Jesus through the embodiment of the gospel. To embody the gospel of Jubilee, we must display the message of justice and mercy in our everyday lives.

In Matthew 5:14–16, Jesus talks about the role of Christians in embodying the message of the gospel in the world:

> You are the light of the world. A city built on a hill cannot be hid. No one after lighting a lamp puts it under the bushel basket, but on the lampstand, and it gives light to all in the house. In the same way, let your light shine before others, so that they may see your good works and give glory to your Father in heaven.

Here Jesus teaches us that we must display the gospel in our everyday lives. Love, truth-telling, empowerment, forgiveness, rest, nonviolent living, and church engagement are all ways we bring light into darkness and become a lamp in the world. The next seven chapters dive into the seven practices of Jesus that we must embody in the world. We must embody the message of Jubilee in our good works of justice so that we can point to our heavenly Father. When we do justice and love mercy on a daily basis, we point to a God who saves and liberates.

Remember, the power found in proclaiming and embodying Jubilee in the world is the foundation on which all change is possible.

Creating Social Change

While in my PhD program, I had to read a book called *Diffusion of Innovations*.[2] It explores how ideas become normalized in a society. Here is the claim of the book: individuals adopt new behaviors based on the influences of everyday people they come in contact with. During my late-night studies, I went deep down a rabbit hole in order to answer two questions.

First, *what percentage of ordinary people do you need to win over to create cultural momentum?* A momentum point is the point where you have won over enough people that an idea begins to spread virally. An idea that becomes viral is like a snowball that begins rolling downhill. Momentum points make ideas and cultural expressions really hard to stop. While virality is easy to spot in social media, I wanted to know how it works within everyday human interactions.

Second, *what percentage of ordinary people are needed to create critical mass?* Critical mass is reached when so many people adopt a new idea that it spreads to the vast majority of the population. Critical mass means you have changed an aspect of culture. In other words, reaching critical mass means a social convention is changed because the new idea was diffused through enough people, it caught momentum, and it finally became a cultural norm. This can happen at your workplace, in your family, in your church, among your friend groups, or in broader aspects of culture like politics or government.

Most people have smartphones now. How did that happen exactly? Southern statues that represent racist leaders are being changed. What were the momentum points and critical mass events that made this possible? We all want better conditions for the poor, workplaces that advocate for their employees, politicians who don't lie, economic systems that foster equality, and churches that refuse to tolerate domineering leaders. Activist Shane Claiborne writes, "The Jesus revolution is a subtle contagion, spreading one little life, one little hospitality house, at a time."[3] These small acts of justice and mercy are the way we are looking to bring about culture change. Let's explore what it will take to make this happen.

Momentum Point and Critical Mass

Before getting into the theoretical statistics, I'll start with an imaginary story in which you are the main character. Imagine you are waiting tables at a local restaurant. The business has thirty employees. Most of the people working at the restaurant attend college and are looking to make good tips while living at home. Six months after getting the job, you notice that there is an older table cleaner (busser) named Andrew who has worked at the restaurant for about two years. While most of the staff gets along really well, you notice that Andrew is pretty isolated. He is in his late forties, has a hard time connecting with his coworkers, and isn't liked by others. Even the managers say things about him behind his back. Your coworkers are always gossiping about his appearance and how strange he can be. You also notice that he has not been given a chance to wait tables, which does not match the restaurant protocol. One night you offer to give him a ride home and begin to learn more about his story. He is divorced, has two kids who live with him, and was homeless less than a year ago. Every day he works at a laundromat, and every night he works at the restaurant. After learning he takes the bus everywhere he goes, you understand why he is so tired and has a hard time getting to work on time. While you are talking to him, Andrew fights back tears while explaining how arduous it is for him to come to work when no one wants to see him.

When you drop Andrew off at his apartment, it hits you. He hasn't been given the opportunity to wait tables because management knows that most people don't like him much. This isn't right because Andrew has not done anything wrong. Now that you have heard his story, you now know that many lies have been spread about Andrew and that this discourages him. Even worse, the managers are pretty weak leaders, so they don't do anything about it. After you get home, you reflect on Andrew's story. You are learning about the radical practice of love that Jesus taught in the parable of the good Samaritan. You identify Andrew as someone who is your biblical neighbor, and you feel it is your Christian responsibility to do something about his situation. You don't trust the managers, so you decide you want to bring some culture change right where you are. How many people need to begin engaging in neighbor love toward Andrew to create cultural momentum? How many more people are needed to create critical mass? Let's look at the numbers.

According to social scientists, if you want to change something around you but are not in a position of leadership, you are a *minority influencer*. You are outnumbered, you want to see change, and you are willing to do something to bring about the change. Here is the question: If thirty people work at the restaurant, how many people do you need to influence to create cultural momentum? Research shows that roughly 10 percent of the population of any given cultural system (family, workplace, government, church, etc.) is needed to begin creating cultural momentum (see fig. 3.1).

For the example above, this means you need three out of the thirty people you work with to engage in neighborly love toward Andrew to build momentum. That is not very many people! If someone engages in Jesus's radical practice of love, it will affect their attitude toward people and the way they interact with others. There will be a noticeable difference among those three change agents in the workplace. When this new love for your coworker spreads organically, we call it *social contagion*. Through social contagion, new attitudes and actions become infectious in social networks. In fact, studies show that behaviors can spread easily without preexisting emotional attachments, and they often spread without rational explanation.[4] This means that you don't need to know someone extremely well or always explain yourself to have a social impact on them. How can you increase your success as a minority influencer? If you are

FIGURE 3.1

Creating Cultural Momentum

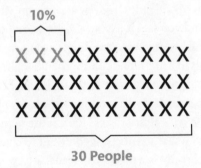

Foundations for Justice

serious about creating cultural change, you should (1) do it with others, (2) display an ongoing commitment to the new cultural value or behavior, and (3) be resilient when met with resistance.[5] These are three predictors of success. So how do you move from cultural momentum to creating critical mass?

Research shows that 25 to 40 percent of the people in a cultural system (family, workplace, government, church, etc.) need to adopt a new behavior or value to create critical mass. For the example above, this means that you need seven to twelve people to adopt the new cultural value of neighbor love toward Andrew to see the culture at work change. When you get to the 25 to 40 percent mark, studies show that the rest of the population (your coworkers) is likely to see loving Andrew as normal. When this happens, love toward Andrew stops being weird or strange, and caring for Andrew becomes normal (see fig. 3.2).

What is the big-picture takeaway from all this information? The way to change the world is for everyday Christians to engage in the practices of Jesus among like-minded coconspirators with the goal of reaching critical mass. Motivated by love of God, worship of Jesus, and faithfulness to his teachings, we should strive to inspire social change. We have the opportunity to apply the example of

FIGURE 3.2

Creating Critical Mass

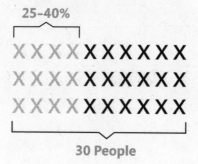

30 People

The way to change
the world is for everyday
Christians to engage
in the practices of Jesus
among like-minded
coconspirators with
the goal of reaching
critical mass.

Jesus in real-world situations and see what happens. James K. A. Smith notes that "we learn to be virtuous by imitating exemplars of justice, compassion, kindness, and love."[6] Smith's reflection squares with the research. Everyday activists can shape culture by imitating Jesus with others, and over the course of time, culture can change.

If you are engaging with this chapter, you will have a lot of questions: Is it really this easy? What if those in leadership resist me from the beginning? What if I can't get someone to join me? When should I take myself out of a cultural system (workplace, family, church, etc.) because my efforts are not working? Stick with me. I will address these questions in a bit. While the numbers make this look easy, fostering change in real-world situations is extremely hard. Yet, if you are convinced that Jubilee is meant for this world and desire to partner with others to make it a reality, there are five concrete steps you can take. Once you decide on a radical practice of Jesus, you can implement these steps in your everyday life. Let's see what the five steps for creating cultural change look like in regard to the radical practice of neighbor love.

Five Steps for Creating Cultural Change	
1. Determination	You are noticeably convinced of neighbor love.
2. Demonstration	You engage in neighbor love on a regular basis.
3. Transmission	You practice neighbor love in situations where people notice and experience the benefit.
4. Recruitment	You communicate to others why neighbor love will create a better culture.
5. Mobilization	You practice neighbor love with others.

We can see Jesus engaging in these five steps throughout his ministry. Jesus was determined to do the will of God in the world. He demonstrated his radical message of Jubilee through his proclamation and embodied ministry. Jesus transmitted the benefits of Jubilee through everyday social interactions. He and his followers recruited others to the movement. He mobilized those around him to get to work in the world. All of Jesus's social interactions were undergirded by the Spirit of God in the world and the mysterious power of the gospel.

In the twentieth and twenty-first centuries, social scientists have discovered what God already knew: humans rub off on each other. We change each other through social contact and are likely to adopt cultural behaviors when we are in groups. People often change when they see something new and mimic behavior—often before they realize they are doing it! The social scientists who study how to create lasting social change are simply catching up to what Jesus already knew and what Jesus already taught us to do in the New Testament.[7]

Three Types of Cultural Change

Social scientists identify two types of cultural change that can occur.[8] I'm going to add a third type of change in the event the first two don't work.

Gradual Cultural Change

The first type of cultural change is called functionalism, which is a fancy way of saying gradual change. Theorists claim that cultural systems like family, government, and workplace have an equilibrium that must be maintained. In this view, balance in the cultural system is more important than change. To keep order and avert chaos, change needs to happen slowly over time.

Let's explore how gradual change can be successful in the restaurant situation. In this scenario, let's say you have reached critical mass and most of the employees are integrating Andrew into the staff so he can flourish. Most people are loving him well. It would be ideal for management to allow Andrew to be given the respect and honor that everyone else has been given. This means that access to raises, hours, and job changes should extend to Andrew. In an ideal situation, you and your coworkers inspire and appeal to the leadership to make this happen. It could take a really long time for those in power to change their minds, which is why those looking to make gradual cultural change must strategize for the long haul and include key leaders who have the power to create systemic change. Long-lasting cultural change is hard to establish without the eventual buy-in of those holding power. Moreover, gradual cultural change will always hit a ceiling if leaders are not on board.[9] In this scenario, you are able to get the leaders to follow through with their policy and allow Andrew the privileges of upward mobility. Congrats, it took some time, but you did it!

Sudden Cultural Change

Sudden cultural change is the second type of change and is based on conflict theory. This position holds that in order to balance the scales of justice more quickly, sudden and radical change is ideal. In these situations, the need for justice is more important than the peace that exists in society.

Sudden change is made through a number of social practices that apply great pressure on a cultural system. In many social situations, the injustice has become so great and the scales of justice are so out of balance that sudden change is necessary to restore justice. The Year of Jubilee from Leviticus 25 is a perfect example of God suddenly changing the economic, social, and political order in Israel to restore justice for the vulnerable. Oftentimes, justice needs to happen suddenly with or without the consent of those in power.

Let's imagine a situation at the restaurant in which your fellow employees are on board with Andrew becoming a waiter. Yet, the managers refuse to give Andrew a shot because of their prejudice. In this situation, how can you try to bring sudden change? You and your coworkers can protest through an ultimatum. You can tell your bosses that if they don't allow Andrew the opportunity to become a waiter, your group won't show up for work on a certain day. You can organize a boycott of the restaurant on a predetermined date. You can contact those above your managers, citing that the work environment is unfair and that the restaurant leadership is not following their own protocols. In these situations, be ready for resistance and be ready to pay the price if you lose. You might get fired. You might be marginalized yourself. You might be painted as a problem employee. Often, this is what it means to follow Jesus. In the event that sudden change isn't possible, what are you to do then? There are many situations in which you can't be in a toxic social setting and change it at the same time. There are times when your conscience is bothered to the point you must leave the family environment, work situation, local church, or social setting you are in. While such situations are often tragic and discouraging, leaving can be the only choice in order to follow Jesus with integrity.

Creating a New Space

When gradual and sudden cultural change aren't possible, the only choice can be to leave in order to create something entirely new. At some point, you will find yourself in a social situation in which you can't function as a Christian. Perhaps there is too much toxicity and temptation that surround you. Sometimes family members are a stumbling block to your faith or are unsafe to live with. You don't have the strength to bring change. Sometimes a work environment is so poisonous that it is impossible to create critical mass. In these situations, you might need to leave. Remember that Jesus abandoned parts of the religious establishment in Israel because the Pharisees and Sadducees were not willing to listen and refused to change. It was toxic for Jesus to be a part of their cultural system. Sometimes, in a similar situation, God is calling you to something new. Often, God is calling you to embody the gospel of Jubilee among a new group of people. You might consider joining a church plant, business start-up, or new nonprofit. Starting something new can be difficult, but new cultural expressions are often some of the best soil in which to cultivate your desires and longings for justice and to engage in kingdom experimentation.

Jesus and Social Change

We are coming to the end of part 1 of this book, and while reading part 2, I want you to keep this chapter in mind. Be asking these questions: When did Jesus create change from within a cultural system? When did Jesus create sudden cultural change? In what way did Jesus break off from the social systems of the first century to create a new cultural space? How do we see the gospel at work in the lives of those Jesus is serving? When does Jesus embody the gospel? When does Jesus proclaim the gospel?

While reading about the radical practices of Jesus in the next seven chapters, consider how they should be introduced to your own spheres of cultural influence. With the gospel of Jubilee, a spirit of determination, the Holy Spirit, and a small group of coconspirators, social change is possible!

Everyday Activist
TAKEAWAYS

1 *Everyday activists identify the cultural systems they want to change.*

Begin to think through the various aspects of culture you participate in: government/politics, economics, work, customs/traditions, family, arts, and language. When you think of the change you desire to bring to the world, what area stands out to you? While you can't be a change agent in every area of life, you can focus on one cultural system and get started. Perhaps it is your family, your work environment, politics, or your church. Pray and think through the area that God is calling you to engage in.

2 *Everyday activists count the cost of following the five steps for creating cultural change.*

The five steps for creating cultural change are be *determined*, *demonstrate* the radical practice, *transmit* the radical practice through human contact, *recruit* by communicating the radical practice, and *mobilize* by partnering with others as you carry out the radical practice. Before you engage in the work of justice in an area you are called to, count the cost of becoming a change agent. Have you prayed about it? Have you connected the area of justice to the life and ministry of Jesus? Do you have a support system either within the social setting or outside it? Are you prone to overreact and stand up quickly for what is right? Are you prone to underreact when you see something wrong and do nothing? If you were to start the process, which of the five steps would be easy for you? Which would be difficult? Do you have coconspirators who offset your weaknesses? Can you handle criticism? These are some of the sobering questions you must bring before your friends, trusted mentors, and God in prayer before you dive in.

3 *Everyday activists discern over time whether gradual change, sudden change, or leaving to create a new space is best for the sake of Jubilee.*

Here are some questions that can help you discern which type of change is best in your situation. Are there leaders who are open to change? If the answer is yes, perhaps you can engage in gradual change. After a year of trying gradual change, you might notice that leadership isn't open to any long-lasting changes. In this case, you will be at an important crossroads. Do you switch your strategy to sudden cultural change and apply pressure that will create a great deal of conflict? Can you afford to do this personally? Do you bow out to create something new? If you do bow out to create something new, are you going to leave quietly or publicly criticize the institution you left? These are all variables that should be examined in Christian community, among trusted friends, and with the text of Scripture open before you. Pray. Think. Feel. Retreat with God. God will lead you.

Reflection Questions

Do you believe that the gospel of Jubilee is powerful enough to change the world? If so, how can you share it in word and deed?

In what setting are you willing to apply the five steps for creating cultural change?

Who are the coconspirators God is asking you to join hands with to create cultural change around you?

PART 2

Practices
of Justice

Jesus' transgression of the "law and order" established between Jews and Samaritans characterizes his ministry. It shows his intentional solidarity with a "crucified class" of people.

KELLY DOUGLAS BROWN

To feel the love of people whom we love is a fire that feeds our life. But to feel the affection that comes from those whom we don't know is something still greater and more beautiful.

PABLO NERUDA

Chapter Four

Love > Fear

Main Thought

Everyday activists follow Jesus by radically loving the vulnerable and marginalized.

Gospel Connect

We are called to embody the neighborly love that was displayed on the cross.

Definitions

Love: Self-sacrifice for others

Fear: Feelings of anxiety or dread

Neighbor: Someone unlike us who is suffering

Mercy: Giving someone help that they don't deserve

Compassion: Feeling sympathy toward someone who is in need

Passages to Read

Luke 4:20–30; 10:25–37; 1 Corinthians 10:24

I have a question for you. Who is your neighbor? Who comes to your mind right away when you think of your neighbor? I grew up considering my neighbors the people who lived to the left and right of my childhood house. From the age of twelve, I was raised in rural Washington in a nice big house around other nice big houses. In order to live in the neighborhood, you needed to be pretty financially successful. Most of our immediate neighbors were firefighters and police officers. The dad of one of my childhood friends was a Boeing engineer. These were my neighbors. Do you have a wider definition of neighbor? You might consider your co-workers, your family, or your friend group your neighbors. I learned very quickly while studying the New Testament that the concept of neighboring is very important to Jesus.

When we look back over much of human history, we see that the definition of *neighbor* had some pretty clear limits. Your neighbor was a fellow citizen of your nation. You fought in wars alongside your neighbor. You voted with your neighbor. You shared local news with your neighbor. They lived near you. They shared a similar socioeconomic background, spoke the same language, and had similar religious beliefs. In short, your neighbor shared similar values, believed similar stories, and shared large parts of your culture.

Then something seismic happened near the end of the twentieth century. We entered a global era.

The last 150 years have boasted the inventions of food factories, cell phones, advanced weapons, cars, and airplanes. These inventions launched us into a global age in which our world has become smaller and more accessible than ever before. Your phone connects you to anywhere in the world. A plane can take you to a different country within hours. You can hop on the internet and find pieces of information in a split second. The average life span is increasing. Culture is speeding up. Borders are being contested. Cultures are clashing. Values are being challenged. We are learning that something that happens across the world can have a real and present impact on our lives. From 9/11 in 2001 to the recent Covid-19 pandemic, we are being constantly reminded how small and interconnected the world has become.

The global era is challenging our understanding of neighboring. In the global age, who is your neighbor? Whom should you take care of? How do you embrace the world without losing your cultural distinctiveness? How do you maintain your ethnic identity? What does globalization mean for borders? What does it mean for nations? What does it mean for resource sharing? How does it impact the church? What does it mean for those living around you? How does it shape evangelism? What does it mean for Christian activism? What does it mean for where you live?

Who is my neighbor?

What is common in this global moment is that many people are afraid. Afraid of the warp-speed cultural change. Afraid that no one will welcome their family in crisis. Afraid of being voted out of office for taking a stand. Afraid that history is being erased. Afraid of being sent back to a country filled with violence. Afraid of the police. Afraid of jobs going overseas. Afraid of online bullying. Afraid of being canceled. Afraid of saying the wrong thing. Afraid of past digital mistakes coming back to haunt them. Afraid of not getting a job. Afraid of being forgotten. Afraid of inaction. Afraid of climate change. Afraid of the wealth gap increasing. Afraid of economic recession. Afraid of losing cultural distinctiveness. Afraid of war. Afraid of children not making it.[1]

Here is the tricky part of living in fear: fear causes humans to limit their definition of neighbor to a small group of people who are just like them. Humans naturally whittle down the list of authorized neighbors when their culture and values are at stake. African

American contemplative Howard Thurman notes that we share with neighbors who "are of the household of my life and meaning and values, and then if I have anything left, then I share it with those who are next in line."[2] The line of people we are willing to help is only getting smaller. We see this happening especially in the Western world.

If fear causes us to limit our circle of neighbors, what does love do? That all depends on our definition of love. We can't look to worldly love. Not modern love. Not postmodern love. Not Western love. Not your love. Not my love. We must look to God's love in the person and work of Jesus. The definitions Jesus provides of neighbor and love in the parable of the good Samaritan are radical. They confront our fears in the global age. They confront the social, political, and cultural anxiety that many are experiencing in the twenty-first century. In the ancient text of the Christian Scriptures, Jesus gives us a blueprint for neighboring that has the capacity to renew our culture with a love divine. Whether you like the global age or not, whether you find yourself on the political right or left or in the center, the incredibly subversive story called the parable of the good Samaritan cuts against our Western understanding of neighboring.

Neighbor Love

In the time of Jesus, God's people were longing to restore a religious and cultural identity that had been chipped away at for hundreds of years. The Jews had experienced so much violence and oppression at the hands of global empires that they longed for an ethnic identity unthreatened by other nations. One core question that divided many of the Jewish leaders of Jesus's day was this: How should Israel relate to people who are different from them? The religious factions within Israel answered this question in different ways. In the opening chapter, I defined culture as values, stories, and expressions that humans organize around. The Jews were finding that their own culture was being challenged on a day-to-day basis by the Roman values, stories, and expressions. This caused many of the Jewish people and leaders

Jesus gives us a blueprint for neighboring that has the capacity to renew our culture with a love divine.

to become insular. For many, the definition of neighbor was shrinking, and we can't blame them. When so many of your own people are suffering, it is a natural human reaction to take care of only your own.

In the midst of these first-century challenges, Jesus comes on the scene. By the time we get to Luke 10:25–37, the Jewish leaders have already tried to kill Jesus. They want to kill Jesus because he has been retelling Old Testament stories about Jewish prophets caring for those outside of Israel (4:20–30). So when we get to Luke 10, Jesus has already been pushing the Jewish limits of neighboring. It is within this context that we learn from Jesus what the love of neighbor really means. Embracing our neighbor as a radical practice of everyday activism is critical to Christian discipleship.

In Luke 10, Jesus tells a story. It was common for Jesus to tell a story to illustrate a truth that he wanted his followers to carry into their everyday lives. Though this story was made up, everyone listening could understand the actors, the setting, and the cultural nuances. Before we get to the story, however, let's set the scene.

> Just then a lawyer stood up to test Jesus. "Teacher," he said, "what must I do to inherit eternal life?" He said to him, "What is written in the law? What do you read there?" He answered, "You shall love the Lord your God with all your heart, and with all your soul, and with all your strength, and with all your mind; and your neighbor as yourself." And he said to him, "You have given the right answer; do this, and you will live." But wanting to justify himself, he asked Jesus, "And who is my neighbor?" (vv. 25–29)

In these verses, a Jewish leader is testing Jesus. The lawyer asks Jesus how to inherit eternal life. After Jesus asks, "What is written in the law?" the Jewish teacher recites two well-known commands from the Old Testament. These two commands are to love God with everything you have and to love your neighbor. The first is from Deuteronomy 6:5, and the second is from Leviticus 19:18. These Old Testament verses were not considered provocative in any way.

In verse 29, we learn that the lawyer is looking for a way to defend himself and therefore asks Jesus, "Who is my neighbor?" This leads Jesus to tell one of the most radical, provocative, beautiful, and challenging stories in all of the Bible.[3] From it, we will learn about the first radical practice in everyday activism: love for our neighbor.

> Jesus replied, "A man was going down from Jerusalem to Jericho, and fell into the hands of robbers, who stripped him, beat him, and went away, leaving him half dead. Now by chance a priest was going down that road; and when he saw him, he passed by on the other side. So likewise a Levite, when he came to the place and saw him, passed by on the other side." (Luke 10:30–32)

Jesus opens by saying that a Jewish man was going from the city of Jerusalem to Jericho. The man was "going down" because Jerusalem sits on a hill. The distance from Jerusalem to Jericho was about seventeen miles, which would have taken a long time to travel. It is also important to note that the trip wasn't very safe. Robbers and bandits hid by the road, waiting for travelers they could overcome with violence in order to steal their possessions.

Jesus indicates that the Jewish man was violently attacked, badly injured, and left for dead on this dangerous road. Jesus, the master storyteller, quickly introduces a tension that needs to find resolution. In verse 31, Jesus tells of the first of three actors who come across the victimized and dying Jewish man. The first person is a Jewish priest. It is important to know that God created the priestly line from the descendants of Moses's brother, Aaron (Exod. 28:1). They were meant to watch over Israel and help the people of Israel connect to God. Specifically, they maintained the temple and oversaw the sacrificial system. They were also meant to be a physical representation of God among the Jews and before other nations. The crowd listening would have expected this Jewish leader to help the dying man on the side of the road. After all, isn't the person dying the neighbor of the Jewish priest? In a turn of events, the Jewish priest passes him by on the other side of the road! This would have been unsettling to those listening to Jesus. They would have wondered, "Why did God's appointed leader abandon a fellow Jewish man to die?" Without stopping to explain, Jesus continues the story.

Next, a Levite sees the dying man and also passes by without helping him. The Levites were the descendants of a Hebrew man named Levi, one of the twelve sons of Jacob. God appointed the Levites to assist the priests in conducting their duties. This means that a second person appointed by God to help the Israelites also rejected the man lying on the road. Those listening to Jesus would have been confounded as to why the two people who should care for the dying man didn't help him. Then comes the plot twist that turns this story from provocative to radical.

> But a Samaritan while traveling came near him; and when he saw him, he was moved with pity. He went to him and bandaged his wounds, having poured oil and wine on them. Then he put him on his own animal, brought him to an inn, and took care of him. The next day he took out two denarii, gave them to the innkeeper, and said, "Take care of him; and when I come back, I will repay you whatever more you spend." (Luke 10:33–35)

The third person who saw the dying Jewish man was a Samaritan. The crowd of Jews listening to this story considered the Samaritans their enemies. Samaria was once a thriving Jewish city in the northern kingdom of Israel but was conquered by a rival nation, Assyria. Once Samaria was conquered, the Jews who were not deported by the Assyrians and remained in the land began to move away from the traditional and orthodox Jewish teachings. They created a different holy site, had a different sacrificial system, and claimed they were the true Israel. The city of Samaria rivaled Jerusalem. Samaritans were also mixed ethnically, part Jew, part Gentile, due to the conquered Jews intermarrying with foreigners planted in the land by the Assyrians. Jews and Samaritans did not get along (John 4:9; 8:48). While telling the story, Jesus made the third man an outsider, an enemy of the crowd, a religious rival, and a person who would be unwelcomed by those listening to the story. Why did Jesus choose such a radical and provocative figure? Keep reading the story to find out.

The Samaritan looked at the Jewish man, who was his enemy, and had pity on him. Who was supposed to respond with compassion and mercy toward the dying man? The priest and the Levite! In the social and cultural setting of Jesus's day, who was not supposed to act with compassion and pity toward the dying man? The Samaritan. The crowd listening to Jesus would have understood that the Samaritan responded like the two Jewish leaders were supposed to have responded. The Samaritan ended up taking care of the dying man by attending to his physical wounds (v. 34), traveling with him to find shelter (v. 34), and paying for him to get better (v. 35). Then the Samaritan went above and beyond to repay whatever the injured Jewish man needed to spend while he was gone. Are you beginning to sense how radical this story was in the original cultural context? Are you beginning to adjust your vision of neighboring according to Jesus's understanding? After finishing the story, Jesus turns back to the Jewish leader looking to justify himself and poses a question:

"Which of these three, do you think, was a neighbor to the man who fell into the hands of the robbers?" He said, "The one who showed him mercy." Jesus said to him, "Go and do likewise." (Luke 10:36–37)

The Jewish lawyer answers Jesus's question in a straightforward manner. It is clear that the third person, the Samaritan, responded in mercy while the first two men did not.

Two words in this story help shed light on what Jesus means by "love your neighbor." The first is *compassion*, and the second is *mercy*. Compassion, translated as "moved with pity" in the New Revised Standard Version, is feeling sympathy toward someone who is in need—even an enemy. Yet, compassion moves beyond mere feelings to embodied actions in the world. Mercy is giving someone help when they don't deserve it. Compassion and mercy are used in this story to help define love for the audience.

The concepts of compassion and mercy are not isolated to this story in Luke. In fact, these themes are threaded throughout the rest of the Gospels. Matthew 9:36 says, "When he [Jesus] saw the crowds, he had compassion for them, because they were harassed and helpless, like sheep without a shepherd." Jesus instinctively had compassion when he saw people in need. Jesus didn't respond with fear or judgment but love and compassion. Jesus had every right to judge the crowds and respond with judgment, but instead he responded with acts of mercy rooted in compassion. We see the outworking of Matthew 9:36 as Jesus responds to individuals with merciful healing (Matt. 17:14–18; Mark 5:1–20; Luke 18:35–43). The acts of mercy and compassion that we see in the Gospels define neighbor love for us in the twenty-first century.

The pinnacle of God's compassion and mercy is the gospel message that Jesus died for us on the cross. First Peter 2:10 teaches us that we have received mercy from God. Titus 3:5 tells us that it is by God's mercy that we have received salvation. The parable of the good Samaritan is embedded within the broader gospel story of God's saving work in Jesus. Jesus extended to us divine compassion and mercy through the cross. In the gospel of Jubilee, we become the enemy God decided to save on the side of the road. We become the enemy he embraced with love. We become the aim of God's loving sacrifice. Furthermore, this parable forms the basis for the type of solidarity Christians are to show toward their biblical neighbor in real-world situations. Argentinian theologian Nélida Ritchie writes, "Each time the gospel speaks of Jesus' suffering compassion, it shows his complete identification with the other's situation; it shows his creative and active solidarity."[4] In application of this parable, Christians are to extend Jesus's compassion and mercy in order to live in solidarity with those who suffer.

To finish the story, Jesus tells the Jewish lawyer to go be like the Samaritan, who manifested God's divine neighbor love through concrete acts of compassion and mercy.

From this story, we learn so many beautiful things about following Jesus. First, we learn how to define love. In the parable, Jesus teaches us that love is shown by providing food, shelter, financial resources, hospitality, and ongoing support to a political and religious enemy. Love is a manifestation of mercy and compassion in real-world social situations. African American theologian Yolanda Pierce says that "it is holy to love others, even when you do not understand them."[5] This parable offers a clear example of an act of radical holiness—loving someone who is not within our own social grouping. Love according to Jesus is socially costly and politically inconvenient—transcending the categories humans create to divide. Second, we learn how to define neighbor. A neighbor extends all the way to an enemy, cultural outsider, political rival, and vulnerable person. Jesus's understanding of love and neighbor pushes the limits of the most generous and loving humans among us.

After reading and studying this parable, I asked myself, Why didn't I grow up learning in church that this is Jesus's definition of neighbor? Why didn't I understand how radical our love should be for those around us? Why did I have such a warped and myopic view of neighboring? Among many reasons, I realized that I was letting the American way and the world define what it means to show neighbor love. I was letting the culture around me dictate what love means and who my neighbor should be. Yet, this parable of Jesus calls us to a love supreme, a love divine, and a love that is costly on all levels of our lives. The chart below shows the contrast between the common definition of *neighbor* and the Christian definition of *neighbor*, rooted in the parable of the good Samaritan.

Common Definition of Neighbor	Christian Definition of Neighbor
Allied with your nation	Enemy
Lives around you	Cultural outsider
Shares your political beliefs	Political rival
Has similar social status	Vulnerable person

In the United States, we often define our neighbors as the people who are like us. They share our culture, values, political beliefs, and social status. We usually organize our friends around these categories. We usually organize our churches around these categories. Oftentimes, our own families are aligned according to these common neighboring principles. While this is the normal way of doing things, Jesus resists the ordinary human way of neighboring. In the same way that Jesus confounded the Jewish understanding of neighboring in the first century, he subverts our understanding of neighboring in the twenty-first century. Mark R. Glanville and Luke Glanville note that "the Parable of the Good Samaritan obliterates the boundary markers between those who should and those who should not receive our love, compassion, and service."[6] Martin Luther King Jr. calls the love that Jesus commands us to embrace a "dangerous unselfishness"[7] that should be shared with those around us. The parable of the good Samaritan also challenges us to reconsider who we are willing to receive love from in a time of need.

In a global age in which we are turning to tribalism, fear, and nationalism, the Christian definition of neighboring is radical enough to change the culture around us. If the millions of Christians around the world embraced this view of neighboring, love would be strong enough to overcome the global fears of the twenty-first century.[8] If the hundreds of thousands of churches embodied in their local settings the love that the Samaritan showed the dying man on the side of the road, we would see radical cultural change in our midst. Conversely, if we continue to embrace the worldly definition of neighboring, we will continue to devolve into political tribalism and reactionary fear. Our love will always be tempered by fear if we fail to accept Jesus's radical message on neighbor love.[9]

Everyday Activist
TAKEAWAYS

1 *Everyday activists identify those who fit the definition of neighbor in their daily lives.*

Look around you. Who are the people around you who are vulnerable, in need of shelter, a meal, clothing, and ongoing help? Who are the people who are not going to get care because your friends, coworkers, or family consider them off-limits to help? The first step in Jesus's radical practice of love is identifying people you interact with on a daily basis. Divine encounters take place all around you, as long as you adopt a new view of neighboring that squares with the parable of the good Samaritan. Pause and think about who is your neighbor.

2 *Everyday activists respond with compassion in acts of mercy, support, and empowerment.*

Now that you have identified your neighbor, how can you share God's love with them? This can mean so many different things. Perhaps buy them a meal, ask them how they are doing, advocate for them within your work environment, pray for them, or listen to their story. Maybe someone needs a place to stay or help finding a job. We should be sharing neighbor love with enemies of our country, refugees, immigrants, prisoners, social outcasts, and those who our community refuses to embrace with divine love. If our neighbor love is not pushing the limits, we are not following Jesus.

3 *Everyday activists fight the various cultural systems that uphold injustice toward their biblical neighbors.*

Below is a visual of the seven aspects of culture that humans organize around. We must push against cultural narratives in our workplaces, in our families, in our countries, and within our own customs that refuse to embrace Jesus's vision of neighboring. What rules at work take dignity away from your coworkers? What stories are shared through songs and movies that put down people who are different from you? What traditions need to be broken in your family so you can embrace the biblical neighbors around you? What laws should you resist in order to welcome the global neighbors who are suffering around the world? We must speak out and act out with the neighboring love of Christ that he has shared with us.

FIGURE 4.1

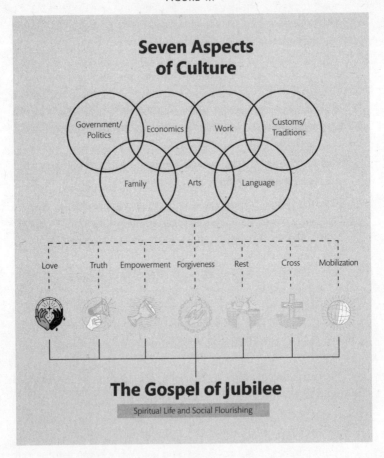

Practices of Justice

Reflection Questions

How can your neighbor love impact the various aspects of culture in your everyday life?

Who suffers mistreatment around you and could use a friend filled with concern and compassion?

Who can you join hands with on a daily basis to defend fellow humans made in the image of God?

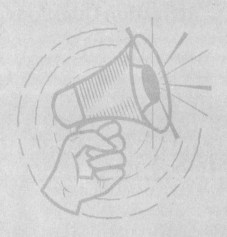

Our environment lacks truth. And when
the truth is spoken, it gives offense, and the
voices that speak the truth are put to silence.

OSCAR ROMERO

The occupants of power are, of necessity,
always seeking out versions of truth that are
compatible with present power arrangements.

WALTER BRUEGGEMANN

Chapter Five

Truth > Lies

Main Thought

Everyday activists speak prophetic truth amid injustice.

Gospel Connect

The truth of the gospel propels us to be truth-tellers in the world.

Definitions

Truth-telling: Speaking up for what is right

Being prophetic: Publicly critiquing systems and people who dehumanize

Lies: Things that are not true

Passages to Read

Matthew 15:1–9; 1 John 3:16–18; Galatians 2:11–14

I n the year 1917, a baby boy by the name of Oscar Arnulfo Romero was born into a family of ten children in El Salvador. Early in life, Oscar worked alongside his father as a carpenter. At the age of fourteen, Oscar felt the calling to become a pastor and began his studies at a Catholic seminary. After World War II, Romero finished his training in Rome and returned to his home country of El Salvador to serve rural communities as a local priest. He became well-known for serving the interests of the poor and speaking truth to power during his Sunday sermons. In the mid-1970s, the government and the religious establishment in El Salvador were oppressing those who were poor, often killing or committing violence against those calling for human rights. A number of pastors, priests, journalists, and others were killed for protesting and speaking out against the government. Romero's weekly radio broadcast was one of the few trusted news sources for people across the country because he never sided with a political party. He often exposed the injustices that affected his congregation and appealed directly to soldiers to accept Christ and reject their loyalty to the state. Romero believed that the gospel of Jesus Christ was meant to transform society through personal conversion and social activism. He embodied the gospel of Jubilee. Romero was a special type of political nuisance because he called out the dictators in power while simultaneously refusing to support the revolutionaries or rival political parties. He was politically homeless, which made those in power nervous. He was often called liberal by many of the wealthier Christians in El Salvador because he expected the church to bring the message of God's Jubilee to those suffering the most.

On December 31, 1978, Romero wrote about the way the larger injustices in El Salvadorian society ended up warping the sense of truth among wealthy so-called Christians. He wrote:

> There are families where the faith is not developed, because what is given is traditions poisoned by economic and political interests and wrapped up with things of faith. They want a religion that will merely support those interests. And when the church protests against such selfishness, sins, and abuses, then it is thought to be departing from the truth, and these Christians, with their children and all, go away and continue to live traditions that are not true Christian traditions.[1]

Romero was criticized by "Christians" who had money, wealth, and status and who did not believe that social flourishing merged with the Christian faith. These wealthy El Salvadorian Christians considered going to church enough. They considered giving a tithe enough. They considered voting during election season enough. They considered being kind to their neighbors enough. Yet, when it came to Pastor Romero holding the rich accountable for not advocating for the least of these in his country, for participating in an unjust military, and for being silent about the killing of peasant protesters, Romero had "departed from the truth." Do you see the sleight of hand here? The gospel applied to the spiritual lives of the wealthy but not the social conditions of the poor and those suffering violence. And if it did apply to the social conditions of others, it wasn't the responsibility of the rich and safe Christians to do something. Therefore, Pastor Romero's gospel was false. It was too radical. It was considered liberal. Romero accurately diagnosed a problem we have with truth-telling. Christians are prone to allow their political loyalties and economic status to warp the gospel of Jubilee to become the gospel just for *me*.

Romero wrote this about those who were unmoved by this message:

> Many would like a preaching so spiritualized
>   that it leaves sinners unbothered

and does not term idolaters
who kneel before money and power.
A preaching that says nothing
about the sinful environment
in which the gospel is reflected upon
is not the gospel.[2]

What powerful words! Romero understood that the gospel must transform hearts and move through the local church and into the darkest and most unjust parts of society. He claimed that a gospel that did not do this was not the gospel at all. Romero applied this truth to the spiritual and social circumstances of his day, but many people wanted him to "tone it down" and speak only about spiritual matters. Romero refused to sideline the truth of the gospel, and for that he was killed. Less than a year after the above words were written, Oscar Romero was assassinated by a sniper while conducting a celebration mass for a journalist who had been killed a year before. He was conducting the service at a cancer hospital among the poor.

Walter Brueggemann writes, "Established power specializes in explanations. But Gospel truth does not wait for that. It rushes on to new life."[3] While Christians in power were conjuring up explanations for why Romero was wrong and politicians were plotting his assassination, Pastor Romero was using the gospel of Jubilee to pierce the hearts of individuals with the actual truth of the gospel—not the lies of those in power.

There is always a cost to speaking truth to power.

Why?

Those in power control the narrative.
Those in positions of authority dictate the truth.
The victors of war write the history books.

While rules are meant to be upheld by the masses—
rules are allowed to be bent and changed by the elite.

The rich control the right to speak,
the forum in which we are allowed to dissent,
and who has access to the lawyers, politicians,
and resources to get things changed.

In the darkest moments in the church's history—
those in power controlled the meaning of the gospel,
defining it as personal spiritual reform while violently cutting out
the social Jubilee that Jesus died to usher into our world.

The truth is always curated through the lens of those in charge.
Jesus, like Romero, disrupted the *truths* of the rich to bring
    Jubilee.

The radical truth-telling that Oscar Romero engaged in during his life might have resonated with some of you while reading this opening story. You can identify with what he did because you didn't come from a place of power. Perhaps you have experienced violence, oppression, and the weight of social sin being pressed upon you and your loved ones. For others, reading about the rich needing to take more responsibility for social conditions makes you nervous. While you may applaud what Romero did in El Salvador, you may have a hard time imagining speaking like that in your own local setting. Maybe you have never considered truth-telling to be something that needed to be applied so publicly. For those who are slightly nervous and wondering why this topic of truth is being applied in a public way, I offer some thoughts on why many Christians shy away from prophetic truth-telling.

Important cultural forces cause Christians to resist the urge to speak truth to power. First, when someone lives a comfortable life and is in a position of power, they often don't think to speak out against injustice. Why? Because they are shielded from the injustices of the world and the cultural systems work in their favor. Those who come from places of privilege end up reading Jesus in a very generic way. They learn that truth-telling has to do with refusing to lie, keeping their word, and not embellishing stories. Telling the truth is about being holy in their personal conduct.[4] Second, many people have suffered so much in their lives that the thought of speaking truth to power does not appeal to them. They have endured so much trauma, violence, and hardship that they want to keep their heads down and not resist the injustice around them.

God understands both the plight of those who have suffered and the comfort of the wealthy. Jesus looks at these two types of people and shows us that truth must break through our private lives into public living. Truth-telling in private and truth-telling in public are both essential acts of Christian discipleship. The first is about living a just life before God by not lying, and the second is about promoting justice in public. This chapter is dedicated to the promotion of truth in public. While this disrupts those in power, Jesus teaches us the necessity of the prophetic tradition for each and every Christian.

Truth in public is . . .

> holy dissent
> the spark for change
> threatening the status quo
> challenging corrupt cultures
> disrupting dominant narratives

Truth in public is . . .

> the Way of Jesus

Truth-telling in private and truth-telling in public are both essential acts of Christian discipleship.

We will learn through the following passage that, as African American attorney and justice advocate Justin Giboney says, "Truth is not subject to popular opinion."[5]

Truth-Telling

To be an everyday activist, we must learn to embrace the truth-telling impulses of Jesus in four concrete ways: identify the false narrative, explain the injustice, unveil the truth, and lead others into just living. In the following passage, Jesus uses the truth to expose injustice in a way that we can learn from:

> Then Pharisees and scribes came to Jesus from Jerusalem and said, "Why do your disciples break the tradition of the elders? For they do not wash their hands before they eat." (Matt. 15:1–2)

Matthew 15 opens with the religious and political men in power visiting Jesus in an area called Galilee. These men ask Jesus a question that is meant to heap judgment on his disciples. The disciples didn't wash their hands before they ate in a manner that was approved by those in power. The Pharisees and scribes reference the traditions of the elders when condemning the disciples of Jesus. While there are some teachings in the Old Testament about washing hands (Lev. 15:11), no explicit commands pertain to the disciples in this instance. The religious elite had created many guidelines and rules, narrowing what it meant to worship and obey God. Jesus knows this. Jesus knows his Bible. He knows the truth of what they are doing. While the dominant narrative established by those in power said that the disciples should wash their hands in this situation, Jesus doesn't conform to the "truth" of the Jewish elite.

> He answered them, "And why do you break the commandment of God for the sake of your tradition? For God said, 'Honor your father and your mother,' and, 'Whoever speaks evil of father or mother must surely die.'" (Matt. 15:3–4)

Jesus refuses to engage with the men in power on their own terms. Instead, Jesus begins publicly rebuking the men who use the law to their own monetary benefit at the expense of vulnerable parents. Jesus asks them why they are breaking the commands of God for the sake of their own tradition. Jesus reveals that the men in power are picking and choosing how the law applies to them based on their tradition. Picking and choosing what is true is a tactic those in power employ to sustain injustice. The question of Jesus relates to a specific situation about children honoring fathers and mothers. In verse 4, Jesus quotes Exodus 20:12 and 21:17, where God very clearly states that children should respect, honor, and take care of their parents. It was the expectation of the law that as parents age, the children should provide a social safety net for them. Basically, God expected them to do what is best for their parents.

> But you say that whoever tells father or mother, "Whatever support you might have had from me is given to God," then that person need not honor the father. (Matt. 15:5)

Without some cultural background on these verses, it is hard to understand exactly what is going on. Here is some background. The men in power were telling grown children that they didn't have to take care of their parents if they donated the family land, money, or family resources to God. This was a sadistic and clever way of keeping resources away from parents who were in need as they became older. The grown child would go to the Pharisees and say, "This land and money have been dedicated to God!" Then the children could keep the land and money for themselves without having to fulfill God's clear teaching to honor their parents. This also meant that the Pharisees could have a cut of those resources. In these verses, Jesus is exposing an injustice that the Pharisees have passed as the "truth" of God. The Pharisees and scribes were manipulating the public laws of Israel in order to keep resources for themselves and enable sinful children to hoard generational wealth. The Jewish elites were passing a lie as public truth in order to acquire wealth. In the process, they were creating unjust social conditions for elderly parents. Jesus speaks truth into the darkness to expose the lie in a public setting.

> So, for the sake of your tradition, you make void the word of God. (Matt. 15:6)

Jesus continues by saying that the men in power have abandoned the teachings of God for the "sake of your tradition." While the popular narrative created by the men in charge appealed to children looking to take from their parents, it was not right or true. Jesus speaks bold truth to power. This truth is public. This truth is cutting. This truth offends those in power. This truth is said in an open forum. This truth defends those who have the most to lose—parents of selfish children.

> You hypocrites! Isaiah prophesied rightly about you when he said:
>
> > "This people honors me with their lips,
> >   but their hearts are far from me;
> > in vain do they worship me,
> >   teaching human precepts as doctrines." (Matt. 15:7–9)

Jesus publicly calls out the sins of the Pharisees and scribes. Jesus publicly tells a truth that reveals their blatant hypocrisy. He quotes Isaiah 29:13, where God calls out people who honor him with what they are saying when in fact they are acting in disobedience and self-interest. Jesus relates this Scripture to the religious leaders who have warped God's just law to line their pockets. He is not about to let these leaders lie about the disciples' handwashing habits when they are lying to themselves.

This passage is one of many that show Jesus's willingness to disrupt the dominant narratives that promote false views of God. Yet, he is not doing something novel in calling out the leaders of Israel.

Jesus is expressing his prophetic calling from within the story of God. Old Testament prophets like Isaiah, Jeremiah, Joel, Ezekiel, and Daniel are a few of many who told the truth publicly in order to recover a vision of justice in the world. The prophets spoke publicly on behalf of God in order to direct Israel to repentance and God's just way of living.

Amos is an example of God publicly condemning the northern nation of Israel for the social injustices that the powerful and wealthy perpetuated on the poor and oppressed Israelites. God used Amos to call the ruling class to account for the spiritual complacency that had led to social injustice. Korean American theologian Soong-Chan Rah reflects on the lifestyle of the wealthy in Israel. He says, "This lifestyle of excessive materialism indicated a deeper, underlying social and spiritual decay. Economic injustice was rampant."[6] Amos publicly told the rich that they stored up violence and robbery in their wealth (3:10), said that God would destroy the extra houses and lavish living of the wealthy (3:15), and pronounced woes upon those eating too much and having too many possessions (6:4). God speaks prophetic truth in a situation in which the ruling class in Samaria had become complacent and were ignoring the rights given by God to the poor, oppressed, and working class. Amos condemned the wealthy Samaritans and later explained that their lavish lifestyles directly impacted the poor around them (8:4–6). Amos was a part of a larger movement of God to speak truth to power, even when the cost was great and no one was listening. When Jesus spoke truth to power, he was part of the Jewish legacy of truth-telling established by the Old Testament prophets.

Matthew 15:1–9 can serve as a template for how we, as everyday activists, can challenge the injustices that surround us. While you look at this template from Jesus, I want you to think about the injustices that are present in your own life, your family, your community, the political systems, your work environment, and our world. No matter who you are, where you are from, or what you do for work, Jesus is giving you a blueprint for speaking truth in public.

God used Amos to call the ruling class to account for the spiritual complacency that had led to social injustice.

Step 1: Identify the False Narrative

The first step to speaking prophetic truth is to identify the false narrative that sustains an injustice. What are the common misconceptions, lies, or half-truths that are spread around you? These false narratives don't have to be political or pertain only to the government. In Matthew 15, Jesus identifies a lie about the law that leaves parents in vulnerable situations. The false story promoted by those in power said that if children gave their possessions to God, then they didn't need to care for their parents properly. This lie instituted structural violence against vulnerable parents.

Think about the false narratives that swirl around you that lead to social languishing and inequity. False narratives are constantly being created and promoted by those in government, by those in right- and left-wing media agencies, and in social media posts. Sometimes false narratives take the form of common wisdom or fake Bible verses. Consider phrases like "might makes right," "nothing ever really changes," "God helps those who help themselves," and "pull yourself up by your own bootstraps." Another false narrative is that America is a Christian nation.[7] These are deeply problematic and dangerous false narratives that allow for and promote injustice. What injustices come to mind for you? What are some of the false narratives that attach themselves to issues and people you care about serving?

Step 2: Explain the Injustice

Next, you must plainly explain how the injustice occurs. In order to do this, remember the imago Dei and highlight how the humanity or dignity of the oppressed is being harmed through a particular policy or cultural expression. Jesus did this by calling out the same religious laws that those in power claimed they followed. Jesus plainly explained the injustice of their thought process. In your setting, ask, How do the actions of these people harm others? How does this policy decision negatively impact my neighbors? How does the anger of a family member dehumanize other loved ones? It is critical that you are able to move from identifying the injustice to explaining how it robs humans of the dignity and respect they are due.

Step 3: Unveil the Truth

Third, point to a passage of Scripture, give an example from history, or use a concrete story that illustrates what truth and justice look like in this situation. Jesus told the Pharisees that they voided the Word of God because of their traditions and called them to plainly follow the truth of God—namely, children are called to take care of their parents regardless of what those in power may say. Jesus did not stop at pointing out false narratives and explaining injustice, and neither should we. Ground your concerns in tangible truths, whether Scripture, historical facts, or modern examples. If at all possible, root your claim to truth in God's Word and the example of Jesus.

Step 4: Lead Others into Just Living

Finally, call people to just living. Outrage doesn't last. Calling people out gets old. Stating the truth over and over can become hollow. Everyday activists must move beyond critique and pontification to right action. So move from calling out inequity to living out the truth. This is exactly what Jesus did across his entire ministry. In fact, we see him modeling the truth he declared in Matthew 15:1–9 when he was on the cross. Even while he was dying, Jesus made sure to honor the law's command to take care of his parents. John writes, "When Jesus saw his mother and the disciple whom he loved standing beside her, he said to his mother, 'Woman, here is your son.' Then he said to the disciple, 'Here is your mother.' And from that hour the disciple took her into his own home" (John 19:26–27). Jesus cared for his mother by entrusting her to John's care before he died. Verse 27 says that John took her into his home. Jesus not only declared what justice looked like but also lived it out to his dying breath.

We learn from the historic witness of Oscar Romero, from the story of Jesus in Matthew 15:1–9, and from the Old Testament prophets that God expects his people to embody the gospel of Jubilee in the world.

When this gospel of Jubilee is not present around us and those in power have robbed the masses of the truth, God's people must speak up.[8] We must shout. We must picket. We must whisper. We must call those in power to account. We must call people to repent and turn from their wickedness and sin. We must publicly declare that Jesus is King and that our sin has led us astray from a God who can put humanity back on the right track. While we may not be prophets, we are called to speak the same message of Jubilee when injustice springs before us, just like the faithful in the Old Testament. We must not only declare that something is wrong but also be the very solution we long to see.

Social Media Warnings

Before we move on, I need to give some warnings for those on social media. In the early twenty-first century, so much public outrage has been concentrated through online platforms such as Facebook, Instagram, YouTube, Reddit, and Twitter. While these are places where learning, mutual sharing, and truth-telling can take place, they are often toxic environments where truth-telling is not authentic. Let me offer three warnings regarding truth-telling online.

Warning #1: Don't Get Caught in the Digital Outrage Loop

Outrage sells, and the internet creates one massive outrage machine. As we click, share, and talk, companies get rich off our outrage. It is easy to get sucked into following organizations or activists who are constantly pointing out injustice in the world in inflammatory ways. It is okay to keep up with what is going on in society, but be careful that doing so does not make you a judgmental person. Problems are easy to point out, while solutions are hard to create. Also keep in mind that getting upset online and sharing a post are not enough. Jesus brings solutions. Jesus gets us off our phones and into the world, where we do the hard work of cultivating justice. Jesus-centered truth-telling will always manifest in real-world activism rooted in love, not anger, outrage, or high-horsed posts.

Warning #2: Stay Away from Mob Justice

Regardless of how much social progress has been made, we humans veer toward the mob. Social media engagement in the twenty-first century can often manifest a toxic mob mentality. Mob justice is a social phenomenon in which judgment is handed down by people who believe they are creating consequences for people who have done something wrong. These people then create outrage amid a growing group of onlookers. Much of the time this is not okay. Oftentimes, when Christians follow the mob, they take Jesus right out of activism. Be wary and critical of this type of online engagement. Be careful of online mob justice; the mob killed Jesus.

Social Media Warning

Warning #3: Recognize the Limits of Online Conversations

Lastly, the online environment is not well suited for the type of conversation that Jesus had with the Pharisees and scribes in Matthew 15:1–9. Conversing about important issues on social media is like dancing in the dark or arguing over a game of telephone. It is awkward and usually leads to misunderstandings. Our apps, social media profiles, and online environments were not created for robust conversations or for authentic dialogue. Can it happen? Yes. Is it likely? Not usually. So when a conversation starts heating up, recognize the limits of being online and try to take the conversation offline and into the real world.

Social Media Warning

I will end with a reflection by Latin American theologian Aracely de Rocchietti from her chapter "Women and the People of God": "The life of Jesus itself manifests and fulfills the expectations of those poor members of society (Mary, Elizabeth, Zechariah, the shepherds) and at the same time is a threat to those who hold power and interpret the history of salvation in accordance with their own interests."[9] As everyday activists, we must press on to speak truth so that the marginalized can be heard and protected. This truth-telling message will be a threat, as was the life of Jesus, to those who want to rob the gospel of its full Jubilee power.

Everyday Activist
TAKEAWAYS

1 *Everyday activists first follow the four steps of truth-telling in their own lives.*

Humans are a bundle of contradictions, complex feelings, and unintended actions. In order to tell the truth with authority and grace, we must do the hard internal work of asking ourselves: What false narratives have I fallen into that allow me to lie, cheat, steal, become complacent, or take advantage of others? If we don't expose the false narratives in our own lives but are always speaking out against other injustices, we are hypocrites and are no better than the Pharisees. Search your heart, unravel your feelings, and explore the thinking that enables sin to create injustice around you.

2 *Everyday activists identify false narratives and learn to explain these injustices clearly.*

I want you to think of an area of justice that you are passionate about. Then begin to think through the false narratives surrounding this issue. These false "facts" or stories will be promoted in the news, among politicians, in your community, or in your family. Get together with your friends to discuss what these false narratives sound like and feel like and discern how they manifest publicly. Identify the false narratives and explain the injustice by rooting your point in a teaching from the Bible.

3 *Everyday activists become the truth-filled solution so others can follow.*

Oftentimes, the greatest impact you will ever have will be in your actions, not your words. While Jesus did expend much energy talking, preaching, telling stories, and speaking truth to power, his greater legacy is what he did for you and me during his ministry, on the cross, and through the triumph of the resurrection. We must follow in the footsteps of Jesus in everyday activism not only in word but also in deed. Let's become the very solution to the injustices that surround us. If you do it, I do it, and thousands of others who read this book do it, we can create a groundswell of just-living Jesus followers who will eventually change the world!

FIGURE 5.1

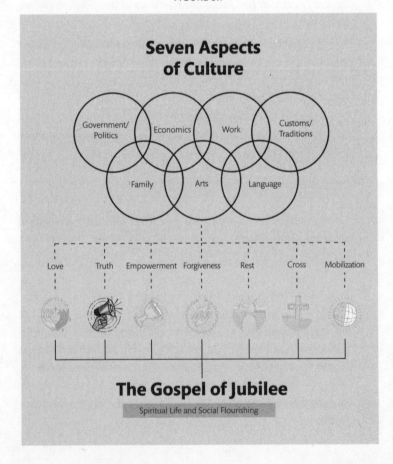

Reflection Questions

How can your truth-telling impact the various aspects of culture that you engage with on a daily basis?

What truth-telling is God calling you to engage in during this season of your life?

What false narratives are you falling into on a daily basis that Jesus can help you reject?

Privilege means some groups benefit from
unearned and unacknowledged advantages
that increase their power in relationship to that
of others. As a result, social inequality occurs.

ANGELA PARKER

He [Jesus] epitomizes self-giving love and
illuminates why we must leverage and
sometimes abandon privilege to further
the kingdom and love our neighbors.

DOMINIQUE DUBOIS GILLIARD

Chapter Six

Empowerment > Coercion

Main Thought

Everyday activists follow Jesus by empowering those around them.

Gospel Connect

The outpouring of Jesus's power on the cross instructs us to leverage our power to serve others.

Definitions

Power: The ability to influence or control

Empowerment: Giving power, authority, or resources to others

Coercion: Compelling someone by force, authority, or intimidation

Hoarding: Gathering and protecting power and resources

Passages to Read

Matthew 18:1–4; 20:20–28; Mark 9:33–37

About a year before starting our church in Los Angeles, I began visiting as many churches as possible to learn about what God was already doing in the neighborhood. My goal was to build bridges, so I met with pastors and expressed my desire to join God's work through church planting. A few of these pastors ended up being mentors and guides along the church-planting journey.

One Sunday I walked into a small church building on a hot morning at 10 a.m. I was handed a bulletin by a lady who greeted me warmly. I turned the corner to the sanctuary and quickly took my seat, as the choir had already begun singing a song. After some opening music and announcements, the pastor stood up to preach. He wore a suit and tie and had a big King James Bible in his hand. I sensed agitation as he opened his Bible to the passage for the day. Standing behind the pulpit, he started teaching. To be honest, I don't remember at all what he taught from the Bible. What I do remember is that during his sermon he publicly shamed church members who didn't show up to drive the children's bus before church. The pastor mentioned that some people lacked a sense of responsibility and couldn't be trusted to carry out a task in the church. Then the pastor transitioned into talking about the children's ministry and how some men had not followed through on their responsibilities. The pastor's tone became darker, his face began turning red, and his voice climbed higher and higher. I remember halfway through the sermon that this guy was yelling at the top of his lungs while church members were expected to clap and respond with an amen. He was shaming people in his church who, according to him, were not being responsible enough with their commitment. The experience was upsetting. I was angry just listening to him. I was sad for those who considered this normal pastoral behavior.

After the service, I greeted a few people as I walked out but left alarmed at the raw anger the pastor had toward his people. I didn't want to walk up and meet him because I didn't want to rebuke a random pastor I had never met. Maybe I should have. I'm not sure. I went home and reflected on the Sunday service.

I didn't like how I felt. I found it offensive. It wasn't because he was speaking loudly. It was because he was screaming in anger. It wasn't because he had power in the church. It was because he was using his power to dominate. It wasn't because he was preaching on responsibility. It was because he was shaming leaders about responsibility.

This wasn't right because the pastor was representing Jesus Christ. The church walked away with an image of Jesus that was angry, coercive, and overbearing toward his people. Yet, this is not what we learn about power in Matthew 20:20–28.

While I wish this story represented an isolated incident, it does not. I've worked at churches with pastors who refused to give up power when the church was clearly in need of renewed leadership. I've worked at churches where important congregation-altering decisions were made without including women and other church members in the process—thus hurting thousands of people along the way. In my childhood church, the senior pastor angrily yelled at Sunday worshipers because they were not fasting and praying enough on the weekend. I visited another church in LA where the pastor called out specific families from the stage for not giving enough money during a building pledge. A different church had five members and a seventy-eight-year-old pastor who for a decade had refused to give up his power or raise up someone else into leadership. I worked at another church where a pastor used his position of authority to engage in a secret affair with his secretary. After I started a church in LA, many people joined us who had been wounded by forceful leaders who refused to take ownership of their mistakes.

To be really honest, I have made some mistakes too. I've been too forceful with others, lacking gentleness or empathy when asking people to do things. I've pushed our team too hard. I've responded harshly to a male leader who struggled with being harsh, thus reinforcing his problem. I've sent emails that were bossy and combative without considering how they would make someone feel. I have had to apologize and ask for forgiveness many times because I did not follow Jesus's radical practices of empowerment, sacrifice, and meekness.

The above illustration was about a church leader inappropriately using power. While this seems to be a big problem in the church, it is an even bigger problem in our families, in government, at work, among politicians, and in our intimate relationships. Power is the ability to influence or control. Power applied unjustly will always result in dehumanizing people made in the image of God. Power applied properly will always dignify and empower others. We have no shortage of bad examples of the use of power in the world and in our lives.[1] Those of us who follow Jesus must be asking this question: Why do so many leaders around us use power in sinful ways, ways in which they manipulate, overpower, coerce, and use violence against people to get what they want? Some people identify the problem by looking at individuals who commit sin. Others identify social structures that allow such people to thrive as the primary problem that must be addressed.

Individual Responsibility

Since the beginning of time, people have used power in ways that devalue others. In the church, there have always been wolves in sheep's clothing, narcissists cloaked as pastors, and people who let their gifting outrun their character. Some people feed off power. They seek attention. Many of these people who are high up in organizations cloak their drive for power within secular business concepts like "success" or "growth" or "winning." Because of their

Power applied unjustly
will always result in
dehumanizing people
made in the image of God.

talent, they get a free pass when it comes to their coercive or over-powering behavior. Others are really charming, so they find ways to wiggle out of their responsibility when people complain about the way they treat others. In these cases, a position or platform enables them to become the worst parts of themselves. Others have a public face that does not match their private face. They treat people one way from the stage or in group communication, but when they are one-on-one with people, they become selfish and controlling. All these situations have one thing in common: a person is using power incorrectly. Anyone who is in a position of power has an individual responsibility to wield it well.

Institutional Responsibility

In addition to holding individuals accountable for their sinful use of power, we must also examine the systems in which they are accepted, promoted, and allowed to thrive. We can point to the way politics are set up, the way government is run, the way our families are formed, or the way businesses are structured that can allow people to be violent or unjust against others. These social structures are oftentimes prone to protect those who sit at the top of their hierarchy at the expense of "less important" people within the institution. Organizations may create policies and procedures that don't represent the interests of everyone. When this happens, it becomes easier for some people to overpower and abuse others—while it simultaneously becomes easier to be a victim of coercive and domineering behavior. Some institutions even create exceptions that favor certain people because they are perceived to be the reason why the church, nonprofit, or business is successful.

Power almost always flows up to the people who are in charge. It is more difficult for empowerment to flow downward. While this power dynamic is normal in the world, Jesus rejects it. In fact, Jesus teaches that power is meant to flow downward to people who need it instead of up to those who have the most. We also learn from

Jesus that those who have power are supposed to protect the most vulnerable instead of those who already have social influence and power, and that institutions should empower those they serve.

Jesus-Shaped Power

Some of us are prone to blame bad individuals while others blame bad structures for creating unjust leaders with poor character. But Jesus does not separate the two. In Matthew 20:20–28, Jesus offers a scathing critique of both the sinful individuals and the unjust systems that do not model the radical practice of empowerment. Jesus addresses the corrupt social systems and the unjust individuals who misuse power. In doing this, Jesus encourages his disciples to create a new social structure, the church, where power flows downward and everyone is accountable for the power they wield. Andy Crouch writes, "The only way to understand power's abuse is to begin with its proper use."[2] Matthew 20:20–28 could not be any more relevant to our current cultural moment. We need to better understand the purpose of power to begin with.

Through the radical practice of empowerment, Jesus redefines leadership, renews our understanding of sacrifice, redeems our conception of power, and offers practical steps for those looking to embrace his way of leading.

Leading up to Matthew 20, Jesus has been teaching his disciples about serving others, power sharing, and lovingly leading others. The disciples think that proximity to Jesus means more power, protection, and authority, and for the most part, we can't blame them! We must remember that the Jews were religiously oppressed, culturally marginalized, underprotected, and violently attacked by many nations before the time of Jesus. Though the disciples were not wrong about the power Jesus could give, they were wrong about the cost of following Jesus and misunderstood what they were entrusted to do with that power. The disciples looked at the violence, coercion, authority, and power of Rome and thought they would need to use those same leadership tactics to overcome their enemy. This is the context of the story in Matthew 20:20–28 that reveals the next radical practice of everyday activism.

> Then the mother of the sons of Zebedee came to him [Jesus] with her sons, and kneeling before him, she asked a favor of him. And he said to her, "What do you want?" She said to him, "Declare that these two sons of mine will sit, one at your right hand and one at your left, in your kingdom." (vv. 20–21)

The story starts off with the mother of James and John bringing her sons to Jesus. Oftentimes, a request from a woman was thought to garner more sympathy or interest.[3] In this situation, the mother of the Zebedee boys decides to privately corner Jesus to ask him one very important thing. She asks for her sons to be at the side of Jesus. While this might seem like a strange request to us in the twenty-first century, it carried a massive amount of meaning during the time of Jesus. Like many who followed Jesus, this mother believed that he was the Messiah, the one who would rule the nations, overcome the Romans, and sit on the Davidic throne. She therefore wanted her sons close to him. Close proximity would secure the future of her sons and their family name as Jesus went about establishing his kingdom. Is this a bad request? From her perspective, not at all. Yet, Jesus knew that none of his Jewish followers, including her, truly understood what having God's power and authority really meant.

> But Jesus answered, "You do not know what you are asking. Are you able to drink the cup that I am about to drink?" They said to him, "We are able." He said to them, "You will indeed drink my cup, but to sit at my right hand and at my left, this is not mine to grant, but it is for those for whom it has been prepared by my Father." When the ten heard it, they were angry with the two brothers. (Matt. 20:22–24)

We may see James's and John's unflinching response to Jesus's question as a noble answer, but what it really reveals is a misunderstanding of Jesus's role in the world. For Jesus, the power that he was given by his Father was meant to be poured out for others. Jesus knew that the reason he had power was so he could pour it out for those in need, and he knew that his security was meant to secure a future for others. Also, Jesus knew that in order to have power over the world, he would have to die for the world. In order to become the first, he had to become the last. In order to receive honor, he had to be shamed. In order to be exalted, he had to become a humble servant (Phil. 2).

Jesus tells the brothers that they are going to share in the suffering of Christ. They are going to pour out their selves for others, just like Jesus. Then the rest of the disciples hear of their secret conversation and become angry.

> But Jesus called them to him and said, "You know that the rulers of the Gentiles lord it over them, and their great ones are tyrants over them." (Matt. 20:25)

Read this verse very carefully again. Jesus uses the example of Roman leadership to point out how easy it is to misuse power. To lord your authority over others is to use the tactics of force, coercion, and violence to get your way. It is to say, "My way or the highway" or "You are with me or against me" or "Sit down, shut up, and listen" or "If you don't do this, there will be consequences." It is a way of hoarding power, exercising influence, and forcing people to give honor. The Romans had structures in which power was stored up and did not flow down.

The twelve disciples grew up among Gentile leaders who protected their power, shamed their followers, hoarded resources, and used violence to accomplish peace. Does this remind you at all of how some church leaders, national politicians, and family members act? For James and John to approach Jesus for more power was to engage in the same worldly tactics of backroom deals, coercive interactions, and power-grabbing moves that are all too common in our world. Put another way, the disciples wanted to use the same tactics used to oppress them to overcome their oppressors.

African American activist and author Audre Lorde famously said, "The master's tools will never dismantle the master's house."[4] While she said this in the context of refusing to cater to the needs of those she was oppressed by, it applies to what Jesus is saying. To overcome Rome, the disciples couldn't play by the same rules. If they did, they would become the very oppressors who oppressed them. The cycle would continue. Jesus knew that to create a just world, the use of power among his followers had to look radically different from how power is used in the world.

He continues by instructing his disciples to look at their own relationships and positions as disciples differently:

> It will not be so among you; but whoever wishes to be great among you must be your servant, and whoever wishes to be first among you must be your slave; just as the Son of Man came not to be served but to serve, and to give his life as a ransom for many. (Matt. 20:26–28)

In these verses, Jesus upends the hierarchy of power. In the world, power and privilege are hoarded in ways that protect unjust leaders and leave people vulnerable. But for his followers, Jesus makes it clear that the real purpose of power is to serve. Power is meant to be stewarded carefully in the systems we create, and it should be used to challenge those who abuse their privilege and take resources while others suffer. Mexican American writer Kristy Garza Robinson calls leadership that disrupts the status quo prophetic in nature. She writes, "Prophetic leadership does not seek to disrupt, but by its very nature it does disrupt the status quo."[5] Jesus disrupted the status quo by using his authority to serve and empower others.

We need to embrace the radical practice of Christlike empowerment in a world that teaches us to take power, grab power, keep power, and use power for our own benefit. Jesus came to serve, not to be served. Jesus came to give his life on the cross so many could receive power and authority through the salvation he offers. We must not use power in a coercive "do what I say" way. Rather, we must follow the radical practice of Jesus to empower others with the privileges God has given us.

What does this mean for everyday activists?

> Whoever wants to be first will be last.
> Whoever has power will give it away.
> Whoever has a voice will use it for others.
> Whoever has resources will share them.
> Whoever has access will open doors for others.
> Whoever is in charge will give a leg up to others.
> Whoever is leading will replace themselves.

The vision of power that Jesus provides is very different from the world's version of power (see fig. 6.1). Ask yourself, What does Jesus-shaped power look like in my daily life? How can this Jesus-inspired vision help create healthier friendships, family relationships, and work rhythms among those I know? How can this view of power subvert the way others are leading around me?

FIGURE 6.1

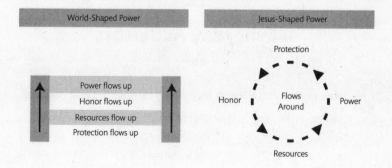

The radical practice of empowering others should impact all the cultural systems that we organize around. When we think of politics, government, family, the arts, friendship, and work settings, we must be people of empowerment instead of coercion. We must be people looking to serve and love in our everyday settings, not people who force others to do our bidding. Important questions should be asked when leading: How can I give away authority so that those I'm empowering grow in their own gifting? How can I share decision-making in my church or workplace? How are resources being shared with those who need them most? If we all embraced the radical practice of empowerment among our coworkers, friends, and those around us who are marginalized, our world would flourish. If we committed to use our power for others, then perhaps everyone would have enough to eat, everyone would hear the saving message of Jesus, our families would be healed, our streets would be safe, politicians would stop lying, the wealthy would share their bounty, and older pastors would be happy and willing to give up their authority for the next generation of pastors. But this use of power and authority comes with a cost. Your platform may not get bigger, and you might not be the one recognized for success. Take heart. When this happens, you are being like our radical power-sharing Messiah. We must follow the example of John the Baptist in John 3:30 when he declared, "He must increase, but I must decrease."

Everyday Activist
TAKEAWAYS

1 *Everyday activists identify their own power, status, and privilege.*

The first step to applying Jesus's radical practice of empowerment is identifying whom you have influence over. You are a part of a family. You go to work. You have a group of friends. You are on social media. These are your areas of influence. Remember, power isn't bad all by itself. It is what you do with power that matters! Who are the people who look up to you? Who are the people who want to follow you? Who are the people being mistreated around you? Are there children in your family who need help? Which of your co-workers need someone to advocate for them? God is calling you to extend your own power, status, and privilege for the benefit of those people.

2. *Everyday activists use their power, status, and privilege to empower and promote others.*

If you follow Jesus, your status is found in following the suffering King to the cross each and every day. This goes against our brand-building, audience-fostering, and power-hungry world. God has called you to harness your potential, your power, and your gifts in order to give them away to others. To serve. To love. To empower. To come alongside. For white people, this often means listening, offering a platform for the voices of people of color, or getting behind the leadership of other people in their local setting. You must always ask, Who can I bring along in this journey and serve? Who can I promote beyond myself? Who needs this space more than I do? How can I share my power and resources so we all flourish together?

3. *Everyday activists fight to dismantle corrupt systems of power with the influence and talents God has given them.[6]*

It can be easy to identify corrupt systems of power around us. These corrupt systems foster evil leaders and create the right social environments for these leaders to oppress those who work with them. To help those without power, you might work for new policies and procedures at your workplace, refuse to support politicians who abuse people, or identify how you can improve the way your family functions. Learn your rights as a student, church participant, worker, and advocate for justice in these social institutions. For example, it is critical that men in churches recognize how their theological systems and church structures disempower women. In *Abuelita Faith*, Cuban American writer Kat Armas says, "It's not uncommon for men . . . to use their so-called authority and their own interpretations of Scripture to silence us, to keep us in what they think is 'our place.'"[7] Armas hits on a critical point when it comes to corrupt systems of power in churches. Men must be aware of these and fight against them in every way. How have you identified improper uses of power in your family, church, and workplace? What concrete steps can you take to foster healthier uses of power?

FIGURE 6.2

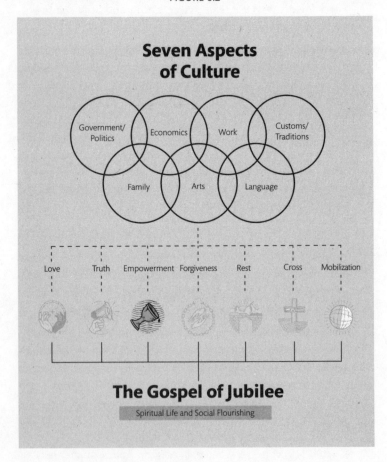

Reflection Questions

How can you become someone who empowers others within the various aspects of culture you participate in?

Who are the people God has brought into your life to promote, empower, and train?

In what ways have you fallen into the worldly ways of taking and using power? How can you make changes to better follow Jesus?

Forgiveness is hard, don't get me wrong. But you have to make up in your mind whether you're going to let what happened continue to capture you for the rest of your life.

REV. SHARRON RISHER

In forgiving, people are not being asked to forget. Forgiveness does not mean condoning what has been done. It means taking what happened seriously and not minimizing it; drawing out the sting in the memory that threatens to poison our entire existence.

DESMOND TUTU

Chapter Seven

Forgiveness > Resentment

Main Thought

Everyday activists are called by Jesus into the radical practice of forgiveness.

Gospel Connect

God has generously forgiven us through Christ and desires that we generously forgive others.

Definitions

Forgiveness: Releasing the wrong that someone has done to us

Seeking forgiveness: Apologizing and asking for forgiveness

Resentment: Keeping the weight of injustice inside

Trauma: Past events negatively affecting us in the present

Passages to Read

Matthew 6:9–15; 18:21–35; 1 John 1:6–9

I have a confession to make. This chapter has been really hard for me to write. This is the fourth time I've written an introduction. It has taken me many months to get this far. I've been back and forth about what I should say and how I should say it. If pages could bleed, these would be red with my longing to do justice to a really hard topic. Let me give you three reasons why the writing process has been extra difficult for me personally.

First, many followers of Jesus already know that they are supposed to forgive others. This command is not novel for most people. If this is new for you, then I'm really happy you are reading! But some of you might want to skip right over this chapter because you know that the path of forgiveness is a normal part of following Jesus. I went back and forth over whether to feature a different radical practice but couldn't do justice to the story of Jesus without teaching on forgiveness.

Second, the Christian command to forgive is often used as a bludgeon against victims who are hurting and longing for justice. In his essay "Restoring Justice," Howard Zehr writes, "We have told them that their anger is wrong, that they need to move on, to forgive, to forget. We have denied their right to mourn and instead have laid new burdens on them."[1] Perhaps you have been told to forgive when you are not ready and therefore are skeptical of this chapter. That is okay.

Third, in the twenty-first century, we are beginning to see the ramifications of churches that used the concept of forgiveness as a weapon against women who were sexually abused. In her book *Prey Tell*, East Indian writer and advocate Tiffany Bluhm reflects on this very problem facing our churches. She says, "In faith settings, a bent toward forgiving male perpetrators is so heavily emphasized, often early in the process of healing, that victims of misconduct, and those who've been indirectly affected by the perpetrator, are presumed to be vindictive or immature if they do not swiftly forgive their perpetrators."[2] This problem is only now hitting mainstream Christian conversations. Yet, weaponizing forgiveness to protect powerful people has not suddenly emerged in the twenty-first century. During the establishment of the United States, white Christians redacted large parts of the Bible that spoke of exodus and liberation in order to keep people of color in their oppressed places.[3] Those who benefited from oppression often emphasized passages about loving enemies and forgiving oppressors when people of color were facing brutal violence by so-called Christians. These acts of malevolent mistreatment still contribute to the collective and generational trauma of so many Black, Asian, Latino/a, and Indigenous people in this nation.[4] The concept of forgiveness has historically been weaponized against people of color to keep them oppressed. While I have not personally experienced this, the legacy is not lost on me.[5] The lack of justice breaks my heart and makes me angry. I could not talk about the power of forgiveness without mentioning the ways those in power have used it as a weapon.

In light of these three points, let me tell you what this chapter is not about. This chapter is not about reconciliation.[6] I am not formulating a biblical pathway for you to come back into right relationship with someone who has harmed you or someone you have harmed. The Bible passage we will be discussing in this chapter, Matthew 6:9–15, does not talk about reconciliation. Second, this chapter is not about when or how to practice forgiveness. The process of forgiveness is highly unique to your specific story, the level of hurt, and other factors in your life that I can't account for. This chapter is about helping us find the courage and faith to forgive so we can be released from the feelings and thoughts that haunt us in the wake of injustice. Join me on this rocky and radical road to forgiveness.

In this journey, we will acquire a necessary tool for our own souls to flourish and to sustain the work of justice in the world.

Experiencing Trauma

Trauma can be understood as past events negatively affecting us in the present. When someone commits a sin against another person, the hurt party often endures a type of trauma. Everyone has experienced bad things, whether big or small, that negatively affect them. Have you been lied to? Have you been cheated on? Has an employer mistreated you? Has a close family member compromised your trust? Were you forced into a situation you couldn't get out of? When we are wronged, we often become angry, sad, or disillusioned. Relationships can be shattered in an instant, and it is hard to know what to do and where to turn. It doesn't take long to realize that we can't harbor injustice for very long. When we hold the sins of others within ourselves, our minds, bodies, spirits, and emotions can paralyze us. Oftentimes, negative effects begin to build within us. Sleepless nights. Depression. PTSD. Overworking. Work paralysis. Undereating. Overeating. Lashing out. If we don't deal with our anger, sadness, and justifiable hurt, they often turn into darker emotions. When we bury the hurt deep down, it often resurfaces in the form of hatred, bitterness, and resentment. This is a very human response. When we refuse to face the past, we often take out our pain on those closest to us. In fact, without the radical practice of forgiveness, we can continue the cycles of mistreatment that we ourselves have experienced. We can become the very thing that we hate and that we have been hurting over. When we don't forgive others, we enter a cycle that oftentimes leads us away from Jesus (see fig. 7.1).

Have you ever been caught in this cycle? God has given us the radical practice of forgiveness to help us break the cycles of injustice around us. While forgiveness does not always vindicate the cry of the victim, it allows survivors of injustice to release their pain to God, who is just to punish those who are evil, whether in this life

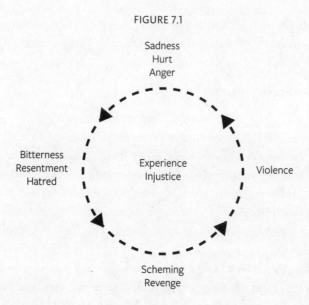

FIGURE 7.1

Sadness
Hurt
Anger

Experience
Injustice

Bitterness
Resentment
Hatred

Violence

Scheming
Revenge

or the next (Rom. 12:19). Forgiveness is a divine release for those who carry the physical and emotional weight of injustice. In an era in which we are increasingly realizing how affected we are by the wounds of our past, forgiveness is a key tool to stay in the fight for justice.[7]

Causing Trauma

On the flip side, have you ever traumatized someone? Have you ever lied to a family member or compromised someone's trust? Have you ever acted with such sinfulness that you can barely stand to remember it? In these situations, we naturally feel shame, guilt, or remorse. These emotions are experienced as a result of acting sinfully in the world. Puerto Rican theologian Orlando Costas notes, "Sin is every unjust act—every lack of consideration for the well-being of one's neighbor, every insult to human dignity, every act of violence done by one to someone else."[8] When we hurt people through our sin, we commit an injustice. When we don't

Forgiveness is a divine release for those who carry the physical and emotional weight of injustice.

FIGURE 7.2

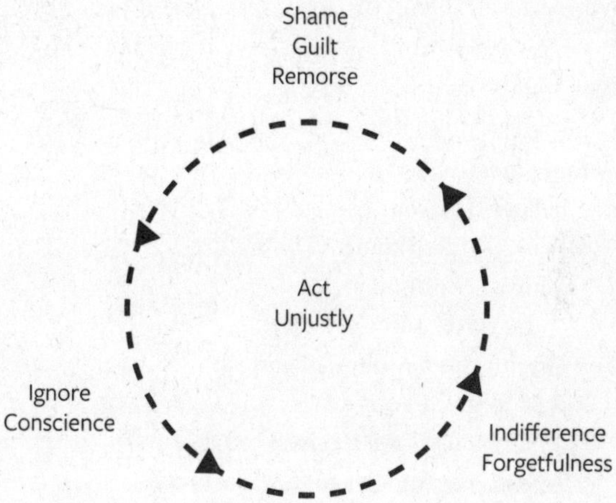

Shame
Guilt
Remorse

Act
Unjustly

Ignore
Conscience

Indifference
Forgetfulness

deal with our shame and guilt, we become accustomed to acting unjustly or we simply hide in our guilt. We become indifferent to the situation we caused. When we don't validate the hurt we have caused, we alienate the people around us. We can't manage conflict at work. We can't build trust in our everyday lives. Politicians refuse to own up to their mistakes. Wars are started. When we don't ask for forgiveness, we enter a cycle that leads us away from Jesus (see fig. 7.2).

Jesus gave us the radical practice of asking for forgiveness to break the cycle of pride in our lives. When we are struggling to ask for forgiveness, Jesus shows us how to release the emotional and physical weight of shame and guilt that we feel.

Forgiveness

Thankfully, Jesus offers us important teaching on the topic of forgiveness. In the middle of a famous sermon, Jesus pauses to teach his followers how to pray. Within the Lord's Prayer, Jesus teaches his disciples to ask God for forgiveness and to forgive each other. As you read the following passage, take notice of the parts that focus on forgiveness.

Pray then in this way:

> Our Father in heaven,
>> hallowed be your name.
>> Your kingdom come.
>> Your will be done,
>>> on earth as it is in heaven.
>> Give us this day our daily bread.
>> And forgive us our debts,
>>> as we also have forgiven our debtors.
>> And do not bring us to the time of trial,
>>> but rescue us from the evil one.

For if you forgive others their trespasses, your heavenly Father will also forgive you; but if you do not forgive others, neither will your Father forgive your trespasses. (Matt. 6:9–15)

Isn't this an incredible prayer?! Jesus starts by acknowledging that God the Father is to be revered and honored by his followers. Put simply, those who follow Jesus should take God seriously. Verse 10 declares that we should pray for heaven to touch earth. We should ask for God to bring salvation, justice, love, and grace into our daily lives, our hearts, our minds, our societies, and our cultures. This powerful verse reminds us that God cares about justice being enacted in the present. Then, after Jesus says we are to ask God to provide for our needs on a daily basis, he turns to something each of his followers needs to do: ask God for forgiveness and forgive those who have sinned against us.

Asking God for Forgiveness

One overarching lesson we learn from this prayer is that we are to be humble before God. This means that God is in charge, not us.

It means that God is the standard of justice, not us. It means that we care about what God says and does. It means that we learn about justice from God. These are acts of humility that should mark a disciple of Jesus. Verse 12 focuses on the forgiveness that we need from God. Jesus teaches us to ask God to "forgive us our debts." A debt is something we owe another person, usually some type of resource or money. With that in mind, in what sense do we owe God a debt?

God has given us life. When we act outside our design, we are in sin. Sin creates an imbalance of justice between us and God. For example, God created humans to speak the truth and not lie (John 8:44). When we lie, we sin before God. That sin impacts our relationship with both God and others. We create injustice within our relationships, which causes hurt, pain, and trauma that make it hard for our relationships to flourish. When this happens, we first and foremost owe God an apology. We owe God the recognition that we have lived outside our design and that we desire to do better. The Lord's Prayer teaches us that we must acknowledge when we live outside our design by asking God to forgive us. In the twenty-first century, this is radical all by itself! Yet, one of the clearest themes throughout the Bible is that when we live outside God's way, we owe God an apology.

In fact, asking God for forgiveness is central to the message of the gospel. Mark 1:14–15 says this about the beginning of Jesus's ministry: "Jesus came to Galilee, proclaiming the good news of God, and saying, 'The time is fulfilled, and the kingdom of God has come near; repent, and believe in the good news.'" In this verse, we learn that the gospel of Jesus comes with a call to repentance. To repent is to acknowledge that we have engaged in unjust actions, thoughts, or desires and that God invites us to turn to a more just, peaceable path—which includes forgiving and asking for forgiveness. Luke 5:32 shows us that Jesus came to help us repent of our unjust actions, thoughts, and desires. Luke 24:47 says that the message of Jesus is attached to the forgiveness of sins through repentance. Near the end of Luke, Jesus has a final meal with his disciples where he teaches them that his body and his blood will be given on the cross for the forgiveness of our sins (22:17–20). The sacrifice of Jesus was necessary because we are in need of forgiveness. Our willingness to ask God and others for forgiveness is an indication that we understand who Jesus is and why Jesus came.

If we are people of justice, we must admit to God when we don't live up to the justice we are espousing. Promoting God's justice in the world without admitting to God when we are unjust is hypocrisy. The only way we can be consistent in resisting injustice is by first resisting our unjust thoughts, our unjust actions, and the unjust desires we harbor in our own hearts. The radical practice of asking God for forgiveness is the bedrock of Christian activism. Asking God for forgiveness also trains our minds and hearts to be sensitive to the injustice we cause because we have measured our actions, words, tone, and hearts against the just standards of God and found them lacking. If we have trained ourselves to follow Jesus's radical practice of asking God for forgiveness, we have laid the groundwork for fighting injustice around us.

Giving Forgiveness to Others

Matthew 6:12 also teaches us that we should pray to God with the intention of forgiving those who are indebted to us. When someone hurts us, traumatizes us, or sins against us, the scales of justice within the relationship become imbalanced. In order to mend that breaking of trust, something is owed to the person who was wronged. Perhaps you are owed an apology. Maybe someone owes you some kind of payment. Or maybe they owe you dignity, respect, or simply better treatment moving forward.

But what about when we experience something so violating that it is impossible to be repaid? Think about a company that steals from its employees. A politician who makes promises they don't keep. A survivor of sexual assault. Those who endure abuse at the hands of family members. The hard truth for some is that Jesus does not back down from or qualify his radical teaching to forgive. Yet, Jesus knows what we are going through.

Jesus was unjustly hunted at birth.

Jesus was unjustly rejected by his family.

Jesus was unjustly accused by those in power.

Jesus was unjustly betrayed by friends.

Jesus was unjustly stripped naked.

Jesus was unjustly imprisoned.

Jesus was unjustly tortured and killed.

Perhaps you, too, have experienced deep pain and trauma like Jesus. Our Savior gives us a radical path forward that does not depend on the person who caused the harm. The radical practice of forgiveness places the power in the hands of those who have survived trauma to relieve themselves of the weight they carry. Jesus modeled this in his ministry and teaches us to do the same. For Jesus, forgiving others is necessary for us to remain aligned with his Father and continue the work of justice in the world. He even teaches us that we should forgive as many times as is necessary (Matt. 18:21–22). Then, on the cross, Jesus cried out to his Father to forgive those who were killing him (Luke 23:34)! This call to forgive people was repeated by the rest of the New Testament writers and became a hallmark of the early Christian community.[9]

In Matthew 6:14–15, Jesus connects the act of forgiving others to the act of asking God for forgiveness. In these verses, Jesus says that God will forgive us if we are willing to forgive others. This is pretty intense. This connection shows us something that is very important to becoming an everyday activist. Fundamental to following Jesus is accepting that we are sinners in need of God's forgiveness. There is no way around this. We need God to pour his love and grace into our lives when we live unjustly so that we can do the same for those around us. If we have truly accepted the love and grace of God, we should share that love and grace with others when they wrong us. To fail to forgive others after receiving the eternal forgiveness of a loving God is to "cut off the branch you were sitting on."[10]

Accepting forgiveness from God is completely connected to passing that forgiveness to others. Are you starting to see why this is a radical practice of Jesus? In an American climate of cancel culture, public shaming, and online bullying, the radical practice of forgiveness is a balm to our society. The checklist below helps us answer some of the questions that come to mind in regard to forgiveness.

FIGURE 7.3

	Yes	No
Is the radical practice of forgiveness easy?	☐	☑
Does Jesus qualify the teaching to forgive others?	☐	☑
Does forgiveness cost us something?	☑	☐
Are forgiveness and reconciliation the same thing?	☐	☑
Do we need to revisit our forgiveness over time?	☑	☐
Do we need to create boundaries after being hurt?	☑	☐
Do we simply trust people after unjust treatment?	☐	☑
Do we work toward justice in the midst of forgiveness?	☑	☐
Does Jesus forgive us when we can't forgive?	☑	☐

Who are the people in your everyday life whom you need to forgive? Becoming an everyday activist isn't just about picketing, calling someone out online, or buying a T-shirt for a cause. It is also about following Jesus in the call to forgive and be forgiven. It is about quietly bowing our heads to wrestle with Jesus's radical call to forgive those who mistreat us so we will have the strength to enter a life of activism and justice. It is about receiving love so we can give it. It is about receiving grace from God so we can share it. It is about living the legacy of Jesus in the twenty-first century.

Everyday Activist
TAKEAWAYS

1 *Everyday activists release their own shame and guilt to a loving God.*

Central to the life of an everyday activist is admitting to God that we are sinful and unjust and that we contribute to the problems of this world. When we do this, we release our own shame and guilt to a loving God who is ready to forgive. By following this countercultural and radical practice, we harness the power of God's forgiveness for the work of justice. Embracing a humble posture before God helps you to establish a culture of love, grace, courage, truth-telling, and forgiveness among those you are partnered with to do justice in the world.

2 *Everyday activists radically forgive those who have hurt them.*[11]

We must take the call to forgive seriously, even when we are not given justice by those who hurt us. Matthew 6:9-15 teaches us to abandon hate for love, indifference for compassion, and bitterness for freedom. We must release the burden of our trauma to a God who perfectly judges all creation, including those who hurt us. In doing so, we release our pain to God.[12] We unburden our bodies for a better tomorrow. So when the pain is unbearable, the light is dim, and you feel there is no path forward, look to Jesus. Hold tightly to Jesus.

3 *Everyday activists foster healthy culture around them through the act of forgiveness.*[13]

There are few things more corrosive to culture than the spirit of unforgiveness. When you are at work, on the bus, at school, or on your phone, you encounter everyday moments of activism when you can practice forgiveness. While grand gestures of forgiveness are few and far between, the small moments when you need to call a friend, text a coworker, or reach out to a family member are always before you. We can create a culture of justice around us through apologies, godly confrontations, and unity-building moments when we clear the air. When we do these things in our everyday stations of life, we help foster a healthy culture in politics, economics, family, the arts, our churches, our speech, and our customs.

FIGURE 7.4

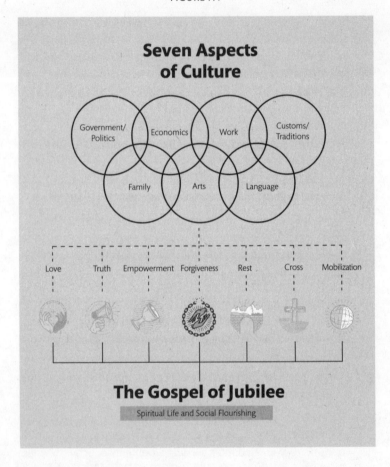

Practices of Justice

Reflection Questions

What aspect of culture could benefit from a spirit of forgiveness?

Whom do you need to apologize to? Whom do you need to ask for forgiveness?

After releasing your burden through forgiveness, what boundaries can you create around unsafe people?

Contemplative practices can be silent or
evocative, still or embodied in dance and
shout. Always, contemplation requires
attentiveness to the Spirit of God.

BARBARA HOLMES

There is very great virtue in the cultivation of
silence, and strength to be found in using it
as a door to God. Such a door opens within.

HOWARD THURMAN

Chapter Eight

Rest > Grind

Main Thought

Everyday activists are called to embrace rhythms of rest and retreat.

Gospel Connect

The finished work of Christ allows us to find rest and retreat, even amid our activism.

Definitions

Rest: Finding peace in the finished work of Christ

Retreat: A divine refuge to commune with God and recharge

Work: Fulfilling the roles of life that God has given us

Grind: The everyday stress, anxiety, and exhaustion we carry to be productive

Passages to Read

Matthew 11:25–30; Exodus 35:2–3; Hebrews 3:7–4:1

have a friend named Nala. Nala grew up on the East Coast, and from a young age, she really wanted to see the world become a better place. She went to law school because she believed that training in the law would give her tools to have a greater impact. She ended up dedicating her life to being a postconviction attorney and policy advocate. In that work, she seeks to dismantle racist and unfair systems of punishment.

While working with Nala over the years, I learned that she felt the world deeply. She was impacted by the injustice around her. While most people could go through a day or week without being bothered by the injustice of the city, Nala felt the pain, sorrow, and ramifications of sin on a daily basis. They were in her body. They were on her mind. They affected her feelings. Her empathy only increased after she gave birth to her child. Then her heart felt even more tender, vulnerable, and permeable to the pain and struggles she witnessed. Even reading or listening to the news could throw off her day. Nala often felt crushed and debilitated by everything wrong with the world. The outrage and sense of helplessness she felt in her body made her start to shut down.

Nala has the heart of a Christian activist, embodying the very compassion of Christ in the world. Yet, feeling the suffering of the world comes with a cost. Through her work, Nala felt a sense of purpose—the time she spent working mattered because she was helping battle injustice. But she was ignoring the signals her body was sending her, and she was starting to burn out. She worked constantly, feeling a responsibility to devote every possible moment to helping others. It felt wrong to take a break or focus on self-care. It felt wrong to hang back and not volunteer to take on more. She felt it was her duty to push forward in battling injustice. The people who were under the heel of injustice were the ones who deserved a break. She felt guilty when things like listening to the news became too much. Has this ever happened to you? Personally, I can identify with her story.

On my journey with Jesus, I've had a hard time paying attention to my feelings and the clear signals my body sends me on a regular basis. Some of this is my sinfulness, stubbornness, and lack of emotional intelligence. Sometimes I have purposefully ignored my health because I thought the good of what I was doing outweighed the physical risks. Sometimes I've ignored my health over the course of a few hours while spending time with those in need. But at other times I've neglected my health for months on end. Whether I've been motivated by good intentions or savior syndrome, it has always been my desire to see the world become a better place. Yet, I know full well that the progress toward justice is slow and painful. I often feel overwhelmed by how much suffering exists and all that the church should be doing, and exhausted because the work of bringing heaven to earth is extremely fatiguing.

If you are reading this book, you might identify with Nala or me. You care about the work of justice, see the connection between Jesus and the work of justice, and are ready to get to work. You feel the weight of a world riddled with sin, injustice, and power imbalances that have a real-world impact on vulnerable people. When a tragedy strikes, you hurt. When someone is mistreated, you get angry. When a church goes through crisis, you are disheartened. Sex slavery bothers you. Racial injustice troubles you. International pandemics worry you. The mistreatment of children and the elderly wears on you. You are upset about the school to prison pipeline. When you hear about war, your thoughts go immediately to those who are in anguish. You care about women's rights. You can't stand that so many people die in poverty. You feel more should be done about environmental injustice. You are anxious about the clothes you buy and the coffee you drink because their production has implications for people who are underpaid. Domineering leaders infuriate you. You want people to know the love of God. You want people to experience the dignity they deserve. You feel the constant pull to share the love of Jesus with those around you. You want the church to be better and do more. You feel the constant need to bring heaven to earth.

Making matters worse, our global age brings the problems of the world to our doorsteps, and the digital age brings the injustice of the world to our phones. An overconnectedness to the world can wear on an activist—someone who feels the pain of the world and sees the need to do something about it.

Our social media feeds us problem after problem,
evil after evil, outrage after outrage, and injustice after
    injustice.

In the midst of our call to do justice, God gave us a divine gift.
The gift is a treasure for the workers of justice in the world.
It is a gift for the weary and heavyhearted.

God wove this gift into the fabric of creation.
Jesus threaded this gift through his ministry.
Jesus modeled it. Jesus depended on it.

It is the gift of rest.

The gift of rest is found throughout the entire Bible. In the book of Genesis, God created the world and rested after he was finished on the sixth day. This is pretty incredible. God built rest into the very foundation of the cosmos.[1] Beyond this, God taught his people to take a rest each week for a twenty-four-hour period. This period of rest was called the Sabbath. Sabbath literally means to take physical rest from everyday work. The rest God desired for his people was meant to give the land rest from harvesting, the animals rest from working, and humans reprieve from a difficult agrarian life. Rich people rested. Animals rested. Workers rested. The land rested. The command to rest was so important to God that if anyone worked on the Sabbath, they would receive a death sentence (Exod. 35:2–3). Pretty intense! What can we learn from this? God created rest to be sacred, a radical practice to be woven into the fabric of our lives. It is a divine declaration that God is in control. It is an admission that God is in charge. It reminds us of our frailty and need to be restored in our broken bodies, weary minds, and taxed feelings. It releases us from the tyranny of the urgent—our phones, our texts, our work, our calls, our stress, and the grind of our everyday lives.

Are you weary? Do you feel anxious about all the work that needs to be done? Have you faced burnout? Are the stressors of the world weighing down on you? Do you have a hard time catching your breath and allowing your body to feel? Do you struggle with permitting yourself to let your guard down before a loving God? If you answered yes to any of these questions, you are not alone.

The incredible truth before us is that Jesus needed a break as well. Beyond his regular rest on the Sabbath, Jesus regularly escaped from the urgency of his ministry to spend time in prayer with God. Jesus also teaches about the rest that we can find in him. The remainder of this chapter explores two main points. First, everyday activists are called to rest in the finished work of Christ every moment of every day. This spiritual and eternal security we find in Jesus is the foundation on which we engage in the work of activism. Second, everyday activists must create rhythms of retreat. These radical rhythms of reprieve are modeled after Jesus himself.

Resting in Christ

The passage of Scripture we are looking at in this chapter comes in the middle of a long section of Jesus's teachings. Jesus has been teaching about John the Baptist (Matt. 11:1–19), warning unrepentant cities (11:20–24), and revealing the kingdom of heaven to children

(11:25–27). Then, in an interesting turn of events, Jesus claims that all humanity can find rest in him. Remember that many of the Jews lived in poverty. They were overtaxed. They were captive to the Roman Empire. They were oppressed. They were overworked. They were longing for political liberation and the eternal rest that God promised. In this context, Jesus teaches about the rest he offers. What does Jesus mean by rest? What type of rest? How is this different from the Sabbath? Let's look at Matthew 11 to find out.

> Come to me, all you that are weary and are carrying heavy burdens, and I will give you rest. (v. 28)

Jesus calls to the stressed, anxious, harassed, broken, restless, nervous, worried, and heavyhearted. He calls out to these people who are weighed down by the world, by sin, by injustice, and by the struggles of everyday life. He says that he will give them rest. While this might not seem like a strange claim to us, it was very presumptuous for an ordinary rabbi to say something like this. In the Old Testament, only God could offer rest for the weary. The rhythm of rest was created by God, established by God, and ordered by God. Our world, our seasons, our sun, our moon, and our very bodies conform to the rhythm of rest. For Jesus to claim to offer humanity rest was nothing short of hinting at his divinity and foreshadowing the blessings of the cross.

> Take my yoke upon you, and learn from me; for I am gentle and humble in heart, and you will find rest for your souls. For my yoke is easy, and my burden is light. (vv. 29–30)

Jesus tells those who are listening to take on his yoke and learn from his teachings. A yoke was a very heavy wooden beam animals carried on their shoulders while at work in the field. Animals were fastened to yokes in order to till the soil. This image conveyed difficult labor and often meant that the laborer was under massive physical strain. Jesus contrasts the yoke of oppression offered by the Jewish leaders with the yoke that Jesus offers. The harshness and bondage of the law is traded for a King who is gentle with those who follow him. Those who take on the yoke of Christ can find rest for their souls. The desire of Christ is for his followers to feel unburdened in their followership. Doesn't that sound beautiful?

The statement "rest for your souls" indicates that Jesus is talking about an eternal rest that we can find in Jesus Christ. In order to receive eternal rest, we must place our faith in what Jesus accomplished on the cross. Paul writes in Colossians 1:20 that "through him [Jesus] God was pleased to reconcile to himself all things, whether on earth or in heaven, by making peace through the blood of his cross." On the cross, Jesus died to bring all creation, including you, back into right relationship with God. We can have peace with God through our trust in the finished work of Christ. This peace means we can have assurance that we are free, we are saved, and we are safe with God! When we trust in the work God did through Jesus, we are justified by our faith and "have peace with God through our Lord Jesus Christ" (Rom. 5:1). This peace does not mean that the world is fixed, our lives will be easy, or injustice will fade away in the present. Rather, the peace Jesus provides is an eternal assurance that God's love rests on us, God is with us in the struggle, and God will make the world right in the end (Rev. 21:1–5).

We rest in the truth that justice was manifest in the work of Jesus, God is using the church to promote justice in the present, and God will send Jesus back to earth to restore justice once and for all. This is the reconciliation that Paul speaks about in Colossians 1:20. The rest we find in the gospel of Jubilee becomes our anchor point for activism. It is also an anchor for when we have our highs and our lows of life. The peace we find in Jesus is especially meaningful for the times we fail. Why? Because we are going to fail as Christians. We are going to fail as activists. We will fall back into old patterns of sin. We will fail to live up to the standards we set for ourselves and others. We will want to give up. In those moments, we need a

The rest we find
in the gospel of Jubilee
becomes our anchor
point for activism.

King who will bring us before a throne of grace to give us what only God can give: peace and rest.

> The rest that Jesus provides in the gospel of Jubilee means that . . .

> > No matter how bad we fail, Jesus pardons us.
> > No matter how confused our feelings, Jesus knows us.
> > No matter how broken our bodies, Jesus strengthens us.
> > No matter what hurt we cause, Jesus forgives us.
> > No matter how shattered our world, Jesus is on the move.
> > No matter how wounded our city, Jesus is her healer.
> > No matter how dark our culture, Jesus brings us light.
> > No matter how oppressive our systems, Jesus will return.

> He will return to make all things new in justice and righteousness.

The work of Christ gives us rest. It is because of Jesus's work on the cross that we can have eternal rest. It is from this undercurrent of peace that we can engage in the work of activism around us. Perhaps you have worked for God out of fear. Maybe you engage in the work of justice out of self-righteousness. Maybe you engage in the work of justice because of the harm others have caused you. Some enter activism because of the false expectations placed on them. Sometimes we follow Jesus out of guilt. All of these motivations will last for a time, but they will lead to burnout, despair, and a broken spirit. Remember, Christ's spirit was broken to give you rest. Jesus despaired on the cross so you can have peace. Take heart. Jesus has overcome the world! The cross and resurrection signal to all creation that we can rest in the work of Jesus—past, present, and future. We can rest in this truth and respond to Jesus, who says to us, "Come to me, all you that are weary and are carrying heavy burdens, and

I will give you rest" (Matt. 11:28). Everyday activists are called to embrace rest because of the work Jesus has already done on the cross.

While this "rest for your souls" is meant to sustain us in every moment of every day, life gets hard. Work can get to us. Family can become toxic. Election season can wear out our hope. Following Jesus into the work of justice does not always allow us to feel that the yoke is light. In these cases, Jesus models for us a second radical practice: rhythms of retreat.

Rhythms of Retreat

Even though we rest in the finished work of Christ every minute of every day, that does not mean we experience this reality in our bodies, minds, and feelings. That is why everyday activists must also create rhythms of retreat. Even Jesus needed time away from the crowds. Let's look at some examples from his life. Noticing the pattern and the purpose of each of his retreats can help us as we seek to implement rhythms of retreat in our own lives. It is almost impossible to engage in the work of justice for the long haul unless we adopt these Jesus-centered practices.

Retreat during Incredible Opportunity

But now more than ever the word about Jesus spread abroad; many crowds would gather to hear him and to be cured of their diseases. But he would withdraw to deserted places and pray. (Luke 5:15–16)

This first rhythm of retreat is one of the most radical. Early on in the Gospel of Luke, the Jewish crowds learn that Jesus is a great teacher and can perform miracles. Israelites travel from all over to hear Jesus teach and seek healing. Luke notes a very curious response to the needs and opportunity before Jesus. In these verses, we learn that Jesus withdrew in the face of pressing ministry opportunity. Jesus retreated to an isolated location in order to pray and be alone. This is such a radical response! Who withdraws when they can heal someone of a disease? Who decides to retreat to an isolated location when they have the words that can grant people eternal life? These verses show us how necessary it is to embrace the radical practice of retreat for the sake of our bodies, minds, hearts, and souls. Jesus teaches us that just because there are opportunities before us does not mean we must engage. He fought the tyranny of the urgent for a divine respite that could carry him deeper into his ministry. How can you incorporate this into your own everyday activism?

Retreat during Decisions

Now during those days he went out to the mountain to pray; and he spent the night in prayer to God. And when day came, he called his disciples and chose twelve of them. (Luke 6:12–13)

Shortly after Jesus's retreat in the face of opportunity, he once again escapes in order to pray. This time we learn that Jesus spends the better part of a night communing with his Father. The next morning he comes down from the mountain and begins to choose his twelve disciples. We learn from these verses that Jesus wanted to get away to pray before making a critical decision in his life.

What are the big decisions before you? Have you taken time out of your busy life to process them? When we retreat during times of transition and big decisions, we can humbly ask God what to do and gain clarity. When we step away for a short period of time, we can separate ourselves from the situation to think and pray more clearly. By doing this, we can make a better and more informed decision.

Retreat during Exhaustion

The apostles gathered around Jesus, and told him all that they had done and taught. He said to them, "Come away to a deserted place all by yourselves and rest a while." For many were coming and going, and they had no leisure even to eat. And they went away in the boat to a deserted place by themselves. (Mark 6:30–32)

At this point in Jesus's ministry, the work the disciples are engaged in is so intense that they can't find time to eat a meal. Jesus recognizes that his disciples are becoming overworked and lack the time necessary to take care of their basic needs. In response, he tells them to come away and rest for a while. They get in a boat to ensure they can be isolated from the needs around them. In these verses, Jesus not only models the rhythm of retreat but also advocates for this rest among his disciples. When things become exhausting, hard, and overwhelming, Jesus teaches us that the divine act of escape to rest is available to us. Moreover, he encourages those with whom he is serving to get away when he sees they are in need of a break. Jesus dignifies the physical, spiritual, and emotional needs of his disciples. We learn from this passage that the rhythm of retreat is essential for us and those we serve alongside when exhaustion threatens.

Retreat during Sorrow

Now when Jesus heard this [that his friend had been killed], he withdrew from there in a boat to a deserted place by himself. (Matt. 14:13)

Matthew records the story of Jesus finding out that John the Baptist, his friend and cousin, has been beheaded. In response to hearing about John's murder at the hands of an oppressive system, Jesus retreats. Jesus gets in a boat to be alone. Jesus is modeling for us that it is okay to retreat when we hear hard news, when we are discouraged, or when we need to express our sorrow to God. Jesus teaches us that we should attend to our feelings and our pain and be willing to deal with the difficult emotions that come from living in a broken world. If Jesus took time out of his ministry to mourn, everyday activists must do the same. We get away so the sorrow doesn't sabotage our joy. We get away so the sadness doesn't build in our hearts and come out in unhealthy ways down the road. We embrace the rhythm of retreat during times of sorrow in order to respond like Jesus.

Retreat after Work

Immediately he made the disciples get into the boat and go on ahead to the other side, while he dismissed the crowds. And after he had dismissed the crowds, he went up the mountain by himself to pray. When evening came, he was there alone. (Matt. 14:22–23)

In these verses, Jesus purposefully lets the crowds know that he is done after a long day of work and heads up a mountain by himself to be alone. Resting after a workday is a practice that we are familiar with in the Western world. After a day of work, we are ready to be off. Some of us are tired of being around people all day. We are ready for a break. The challenge in these verses is that Jesus doesn't get on his phone, go out with friends, or binge-watch a TV show. While I am not saying there is something wrong with these forms of retreat, Jesus shows us that it is good to take time to be alone without people and without our digital touch points. Silence is found in the walk up the mountain. Solitude is found in sitting down by yourself. Beauty is found in patiently watching the sunset. Many of us are afraid to be alone with our thoughts and our desires. Yet, the radical practice of retreat presupposes that we can handle an evening without social media or people. We must be alone to open up our hearts to the divine voice of God.

Retreat during Despair

He came out and went, as was his custom, to the Mount of Olives; and the disciples followed him. When he reached the place, he said to them, "Pray that you may not come into the time of trial." Then he withdrew from them about a stone's throw, knelt down, and prayed. (Luke 22:39–41)

Luke records the last hours of Jesus's life before he is killed. Jesus goes to a place where he regularly prayed. He brings his disciples, gives them some instructions, and then walks away from them in order to have privacy. Jesus prays to God, expressing his anguish regarding the road before him. We learn from this final rhythm of retreat that when facing despair, extreme hardship, or misery, we can find a hidden place to pour out our hearts to a God who will hear us.

These six rhythms of retreat strike at the very heart of Christian activism. Without them, you will burn out. You will open yourself up to unneeded temptation. You will turn into the very person you are fighting against. Your relationship with God will wane. With this radical practice, you will become the very best version of yourself. You will give out of your abundance. You will fight injustice with a fountain of peace and love. We need Christian activists with the humility to embrace Jesus's radical practices of rest and retreat. We must remember that these radical practices were instituted by Christ as divine acts of resistance.[2] Through rest and retreat, we resist the hustle, the hurry, and the everyday grind for something far greater. Through these practices, we embrace our very design. We embrace the rhythm of creation that ebbs and flows between sun and moon, between rain and shine, between land and sea, between work and rest. We learn from our Lord and leader Jesus that retreat is holy. Rest is divine.

Everyday Activist
TAKEAWAYS

1 *Everyday activists show their trust in the finished work of Christ by embracing times of rest.*

We express our trust in the gospel by resting. We show our faith in Jesus by trusting that rest is an important act of worship so we can stay in the fight for justice. We trust that on the cross Jesus already took on the burden of the world. While we enter into God's work to bring heaven to earth right now, we continue to trust in God's divine command to rest. Have you accepted the eternal rest Jesus has offered you? Do you trust the promise that all things will be made new—including you?

2 *Everyday activists pay attention to their emotional, physical, and spiritual needs through the radical practice of rest.*

We are called, as everyday activists, to follow Jesus's teachings on rest. It is okay to set personal boundaries. It is okay to seek out mental health professionals. It is okay to meet with a counselor. It is okay to pay attention to the mind, heart, feelings, and body that God gave you.[3] How are you seeking out soul-supporting help? Are you attentive to your own emotional and physical needs during the day? If not, what will it take for you to begin attending to those needs? If so, how can you help others around you listen to their bodies and feelings better?

3 *Everyday activists practice Jesus's rhythms of retreat to stay engaged in the fight for the long haul.*

The Gospel writers show Jesus engaging in many rhythms of retreat. We learned that Jesus retreated when he had to make an important decision, when exhausted, when sad, after work, while turning down opportunities, and during despair. These six examples serve as a jumping-off point for everyday activists. These rhythms of retreat allow us to process our day, our week, and the volatile seasons of our lives. Have you created margin for these divine rhythms of retreat?

Where will you go? What will you set aside to make it happen? Will you leave your phone at home? Will you bring a book? Will you create something beautiful between you and God? These questions will lead you down a fulfilling journey that will only enhance the work you are doing in the world.

FIGURE 8.1

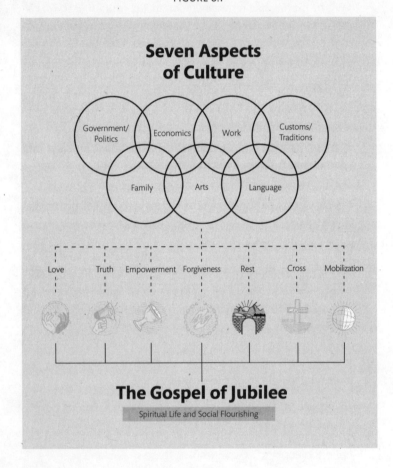

Reflection Questions

How can you lead others into the eternal rest of God?

Which of the six types of retreat can you introduce into your life?

How can rest become an anchor point for the work of activism you are engaged in?

There is no life to be found in violence. Every act of violence brings us closer to death.

BELL HOOKS

Christians must face the cross as the terrible tragedy it was and discover in it, through faith and repentance, the liberating joy of eternal salvation. But we cannot find liberating joy in the cross by spiritualizing it, by taking away its message of justice in the midst of powerlessness, suffering, and death.

JAMES H. CONE

Chapter Nine

Cross > Sword

Main Thought

Everyday activists are called to embrace a lifestyle of nonviolence.

Gospel Connect

God's salvific act of nonviolent resistance on the cross is our greatest weapon in the fight for justice.

Definitions

Violence: Violating the dignity of people through the use of force

Nonviolence: Noncoercive tactics to promote justice in the world

Resistance: Fighting people and structures that dehumanize people

Cross: The method of salvation and the model for Christian living

Sword: Using violence to create peace

Passages to Read

Matthew 5:38–46; Luke 23:33–46; Romans 12:14–21

A few years ago, I read a groundbreaking book called *Why Civil Resistance Works: The Strategic Logic of Nonviolent Conflict*. In this book, two political scientists named Erica Chenoweth and Maria J. Stephan look at 323 civil conflicts between 1900 and 2006. They examine which conflicts succeeded, which didn't work, and why. Specifically, they analyze the differences between a set of nonviolent and violent conflicts. Through their research, they conclude, "Between 1900 and 2006, nonviolent resistance campaigns were nearly twice as likely to achieve full or partial success as their violent counterparts."[1] This means that if you practice nonviolence when resisting an unjust government, you have a 53 percent chance of success. When a group of people use violence to fight the government, they have a 26 percent chance of success. Nonviolent campaigns have a better chance of getting government forces to defect. Nonviolent campaigns offer a higher probability that democracy will work. Nonviolence has been proven to win over the masses faster than violent revolution. Do you believe these statistics? While reading the book, I had my doubts. I had a hard time processing the authors' conclusions. I didn't grow up viewing the world this way. I grew up learning that the sword is a necessary and good tool for justice. All I had ever learned was that violence is necessary in the fight for justice. I asked myself, Why do I think this?

It is critical for us to explore the forces, stories, and cultural values that have kept the church away from Jesus's radical teachings on nonviolence.[2] The violence woven into US history and my own family story makes it hard for me to accept the truth that at the foundation of my very salvation, God used nonviolent resistance in the face of overwhelming force to set me on a discipleship path of nonviolent resistance. Let's go on this journey together.

Stories Woven with Violence

I come from a long line of cowboys, blue-collar entrepreneurs, bookies, oilmen, and farmers. The Buck family fought in the Revolutionary War, for the Confederacy in the Civil War, in World War I, in World War II, and in the Korean War. My grandfather John Brake on my mom's side worked on stealth bombers in the 1970s. My grandfather Wayne Buck joined the navy right out of high school. The military is a point of pride in our family. A rite of passage for a young Buck is owning and shooting a gun. From a young age, I had toy guns that I used to reenact shoot-outs with Native Americans, whom I learned to views as savages. When I was ten, my dad sat me down and told me that if anyone ever picked on me and wanted to fight, it was okay for me to punch them in the face to defend myself. I grew up reading Tom Clancy and reenacting D-Day while playing video games. I looked up to Thor, Batman, and Superman—who always solved the problem of evil through the clever and brutal use of violence. I watched Popeye defend his lady by growing muscles and beating up Bluto. I learned in school from Christian teachers that battlefields should be considered holy, set-apart, and sacred places. As a teenager, I watched from the back of my freshman math class as planes flew into the World Trade Center. I was shocked. I saw our church rally behind the fury of a Christian president who was bringing some type of justice to Iraq. Words like *God, country, freedom, Bible,* and *violence* were brought together as strange bedfellows to reassure us church folk that God was on our side. I remember being proud of President Bush. Proud of his faith. Proud he was from Texas like my family. Proud that he used his Christian influence to bring the wrath of God upon an axis of evil. I bought into the rhetoric. All this can be summed up by a culture of the sword. A culture that promotes the myth that violence is necessary for peace to exist. A culture drowning in the myth of redemptive violence.[3]

In all my learning at church, it never occurred to me that Jesus rejected violence. While the cross was a regular feature of Sunday school classes and sanctuaries, it wasn't an emblem for everyday living. Instead, the cross was merely a symbol of my personal salvation. It never occurred to me that violence was not the answer when it came to evil in the world. It never occurred to me that Jesus offers us a more radical path to changing the world. After all, violence was deeply embedded in my family story. Growing up as a white, patriotic cowboy kid from Texas, I had no imagination whatsoever for nonviolent solutions to conflict. My imagination, for better or worse, was filled with men using a sword, knife, flying bat star, gun, tank, atom bomb, fist, or army to overcome evil. This was somehow connected to my faith. Without anyone sitting me down to explain these things, the cumulative stories, habits, and cultural expressions amounted to a story woven with violence.

For many in the United States, violence has been forced upon them through unjust immigration policies, brutal police tactics, the school to prison pipeline, patronizing truces with Native Americans, Native American reeducation camps, the slave trade, burning crosses, Jim Crow laws, and redlining, just to name a few. While we consider ourselves an advanced Western society, the webbed legacies of violence are embedded in our structures and weigh heavy on our land. Violence weighs heavy especially on those on the margins of US society.

Beyond the societal and structural violence described above, violence touches almost everyone on a personal level. Have you been overly aggressive before? Have you ever shouted someone down? Have you ever bullied someone? Have you ever overreacted in rage? Have you ever fantasized about hurting someone? Have you ever cussed someone out? Have you ever stood by while someone was getting hurt and done nothing? Have you ever intimidated someone into submitting to your desires? Unfortunately, I need to answer yes to some of these questions. French West Indian psychiatrist Frantz Fanon notes that "everybody has violence on their minds and the question is not so much responding to violence with more violence but rather how to defuse the crisis."[4] How do we address the problem of violence with everyday activism?

If you struggle with violence, know that Jesus died a violent death to help you walk away from violence. Jesus shows us how to drop our sword to pick up our cross.

Perhaps you are a survivor or victim of ongoing brutality. Whether intimidation, bullying, emotional or physical abuse, ongoing cruelty, or something sexual in nature, violence is all around us. You and I don't need to have a PhD in psychology or become a trauma counselor to know that the effects of violence destroy lives, break families, tear apart churches, and draw us away from Jesus. Yet, we can't seem to get rid of cruelty or find the courage to stand up to those who commit violence. Violence is ever before us, always knocking and pushing itself into our lives. Violence is a corrosive and dehumanizing thread woven through our stories. The sword is forever before us, luring us to use violence to create peace.

While reading Luke 4:16–21, we must ask ourselves, Does violence fit into the work of Jubilee? Anyone taking the New Testament seriously will come to the conclusion that it does not.[5]

The Cross

In the beginning section of this chapter, we learned from the research that nonviolent resistance works better than violence to incite positive social change. We also know that violence is highly destructive in our personal lives and in our communities. While we have the knowledge that violence doesn't work very well to create justice, oftentimes it doesn't make a difference. Why do we often resort to violence? Why do we explain away Jesus's teaching on nonviolence? It is because we live in violent times, are bathed in violent stories, watch violent movies, reenact violent wars, celebrate violent soldiers, endure violent family members, and are married to national narratives of violence. Yet, we know better! The wisdom buried deep within the recesses of the gospel and on the surface of the story is this: the tool God used to save the world is the same tool meant to be used in the fight for justice. If the sword represents violent action in the pursuit of justice, the cross has become the Christian symbol of nonviolent love. From Jesus, we learn that the cross is the method God uses to save us and also the model for Christian living.

The Method of Salvation

The Scriptures teach that God used the cross to provide salvation for all who believe. We learn from the New Testament that Jesus came to remove the sins of the world through the shedding of his blood on the cross, which saves us from despair, pain, sin, and a life without God (1 Cor. 1:17–18; Eph. 2:16). The debt we owed God was canceled through the sacrifice of Jesus on the cross, and now we have been reconciled to our Father (Col. 2:14). This is Jubilee! Christians must announce these facts of the gospel to the world. Yet, the cross is so much more than the method God used to save the world.

The Model for Christian Living

The cross is also a model for Christian living in the world. Jesus taught and modeled nonviolence, and the disciples applied it as they sought to bring justice to the world.

JESUS TAUGHT IT

In Matthew 5:38–46, Jesus teaches his followers to abandon violence as a tool of justice in the world. Jesus gives five real-world situations whereby he instructs his followers to resist being violent and to love their enemies.

You have heard that it was said, "An eye for an eye and a tooth for a tooth." But I say to you, Do not resist an evildoer. But if anyone strikes you on the right cheek, turn the other also; and if anyone wants to sue you and take your coat, give your cloak as well; and if anyone forces you to go one mile, go also the second mile. Give to everyone who begs from you, and do not refuse anyone who wants to borrow from you. (vv. 38–42)

In this passage, Jesus subverts the Old Testament law's command to repay injustice with an eye for an eye and calls his followers to reimagine conflict in nonviolent terms.[6] Even though retaliation was acceptable in these situations, Jesus presents a different way to resolve conflict. In telling his followers to turn the other cheek and go an extra mile, Jesus offers a deeper and more profound command: respond to violence and conflict with nonviolent, merciful action.

You have heard that it was said, "You shall love your neighbor and hate your enemy." But I say to you, Love your enemies and pray for those who persecute you, so that you may be children of your Father in heaven; for he makes his sun rise on the evil and on the good, and sends rain on the righteous and on the unrighteous. (vv. 43–45)

The main message in this passage is that we must love and pray for those who hurt us.[7] These verses do not mean that we must endure abuse in all circumstances, nor do they say we must stay in violent relationships. Rather, Jesus is helping us imagine a world in which love replaces hate, grace replaces law, amity replaces hostility, and persuasion replaces coercion. Jesus highlights that we can't love someone and be violent toward them at the same time. In fact, the sword is antithetical to the cross. Followers of Jesus can't swing a sword in one hand and hold a cross in the other.

JESUS MODELED IT

Jesus didn't just teach about nonviolence. Jesus also modeled non-violence in his ministry. Jesus had many opportunities to be violent toward people, but he refused. When the disciples became angry at the crowds who rejected Jesus and wanted to call down destruction, Jesus rebuked James and John for that line of thinking (Luke 9:51–56). He also rebuked Peter when he took out a sword to defend Jesus as he was being falsely arrested (John 18:8–11). Jesus called Matthew to leave a job that enforced structural violence against the Jews (Matt. 9:9–13). While Jewish zealots embraced violent terrorism against the Roman state, Jesus purposefully called Simon out of that lifestyle to follow him (Mark 3:18). Ultimately, Jesus submitted himself to a violent death when he had every right to overthrow Rome with force (Luke 23:33–46). In the most stunning turn of events, Jesus cried out to his Father on the cross to forgive those who were crucifying him (23:34). Jesus rejected the worldly path of violence to accomplish peace by giving up his life. Jesus did this even though he had every right to use violence against his enemies.

While the nonviolence of the cross is a singular event that can't be replicated, there are a few biblical reasons why the cross became a template for Christians. First, Jesus taught on this subject directly to his disciples. He expected nonviolence to be normative for everyone who follows him. Second, the disciples understood Jesus's teachings on nonviolence to be normative for the churches they founded. The disciples and early church movement understood the cross to be more than a one-time salvific event. After followers of Jesus were saved by the work of the cross, it was meant to shape their community ethics.

THE DISCIPLES APPLIED IT

Based on the teachings and example of Jesus, the disciples knew that to follow Jesus was to live nonviolently in the world.[8] The disciples taught that violence is not the answer to fighting injustice or resolving disputes. They rejected violence toward the state (Rom 12:17–21), violence toward coworkers (1 Pet. 2:18–25), and sexual violence toward a spouse (1 Cor. 7:1–6). The early church embodied this nonviolent way of life in the world.[9] One Christian theologian writes, "The early Christians took Jesus at his word, and

Practices of Justice

understood his inculcations of gentleness and non-resistance in their literal sense. They closely identified their religion with peace; they strongly condemned war for the bloodshed which it involved."[10] The disciples' teachings on nonviolence changed the minds and hearts of early Christians who were constantly tempted to use force.[11] Korean American theologian Wonhee Anne Joh writes, "Revolutionary change, as practiced for example by Jesus, must inherently embody a love ethic that includes the enemy."[12]

Followers of Jesus must replace the discipleship of the sword with the discipleship of the cross. The blood of the sword creates more injustice and a faux peace that does not last. The blood of the cross created for our world a new beginning, a liberative Jubilee through which we go into the world to create justice through nonviolent action. This means that, as African American theologian Dennis R. Edwards notes, "violence can never be an ultimate solution to injustice. Violence is not the way of Jesus, even if it appears to be the most advantageous strategy."[13]

Five Principles of Cross-Shaped Activism

Jesus taught and modeled nonviolence, and the disciples applied it within their social settings. This background is the foundation for five principles of cross-shaped activism that must undergird our work of justice in the world. No matter how counterintuitive, no matter how otherworldly, and no matter how much these teachings cut against our culture, we must embrace the cross as we strive to create a just world.

While we do justice and mercy in the world, these cross-shaped practices help temper and inform our activism. These principles help us move beyond the belief that the cross just saves to the conviction that the cross is our model for Christian living. Theologian William T. Cavanaugh writes, "The church's job is to try to discern in each concrete circumstance how best to embody the politics of the cross in a suffering world."[14] These five principles aim to do just that—reveal for the world in concrete ways what it means to be cross-shaped people.

Cross-Shaped Activism Restores Dignity

Cross-shaped activism declares that everyone we encounter deserves the full measure of dignity and respect afforded them by the imago Dei. So much of what Jesus does in the four Gospels is reteaching those who were familiar with the book of Genesis what it means to treat all people as image bearers of God. Simply because someone violates humans through violence does not mean that followers of Jesus can dehumanize them in return. We must dignify everyone, even our enemies. When Jesus refused to call down violence on the Samaritans, he dignified people who had been robbed of their humanity (Luke 9:51–56). When Jesus healed a Roman soldier, he offered respect for a fellow human (Matt. 8:5–13). When Jesus allowed an enemy tax collector to join his inner circle, he granted Matthew the dignity of undeserved inclusion (9:9–13). When Jesus asked God to forgive those who were crucifying him, he extended respect for them as image bearers of the divine (Luke 23:34). When Jesus diffused a violent stoning through nonviolent de-escalation, he restored the humanity of the woman caught in adultery (John 8:1–8). The cross-shaped activist must reject any tool that dehumanizes those they are working against. Cross-shaped activism seeks to restore respect for all people, even those we are fighting against.

Cross-Shaped Activism Tempers Tactics

When we engage in the work of activism, Jesus does not allow us to seek Jubilee through tactics of coercion, intimidation, bullying, or violence. From the beginning, Jesus made it clear that while many tactics for justice are appropriate, the way of the cross helps temper the use of force among his followers. Jesus engaged in evangelism without forcing conversions. Jesus argued with those in power without resorting to violence. Jesus healed people with gentleness and used prayer as a weapon against evil. Jesus refused to allow violence to enter into his movement in order to maintain the dignity and humanity of everyone he came in contact with. When we engage in the work of justice in the world, we must refuse to be corrupted by the tactics of those who oppress. Jesus showed us how to temper our tactics. To embody the way of the cross, we must never resort to the methods of the sword to accomplish peace.[15]

Cross-Shaped Activism Resists Injustice

Cross-shaped activists must use nonviolence as the means of fighting injustice. While the world thinks that the cross is weak and that nonviolence is a feeble strategy for social change, Jesus shows us how to harness the power of nonviolence to resist injustice. While Jesus suffered violently on the cross, he was actively offering protection, safety, and honor to those who would one day call upon his name to be saved. Jesus resisted and fought the forces of darkness through his sacrifice. Through Jesus's nonviolent resistance, he "disarmed the rulers and authorities and made a public example of them, triumphing over them" (Col. 2:15). In this divine paradox, Jesus surrendered to death to overcome it. Jesus willingly died a violent death to overcome violence. Jesus resisted the forces of darkness that stood in the way of salvation to bring us into the light (1 Pet. 2:9).

The spiritual truth buried deep in the foundations of the world has been shown to be true time and time again. The nonviolent resistance of Martin Luther King Jr. during the civil rights movement, Gandhi's work in overcoming the British in India, and Cesar Chavez's fight for workers' rights are all recent examples of nonviolence being applied in history. Beyond these isolated historical examples, activists and scholars have shown that between 1900 and 2006, nonviolence has been more successful than violence in creating social change in our world.[16] Cross-shaped activists must envision nonviolent action as the means of resisting injustice.[17]

Cross-Shaped Activism Expresses Solidarity

Cross-shaped activists enter into the suffering of those who have been marginalized through the spiritual practice of nonviolence. The incarnation of God through Christ is the greatest act of solidarity in human history. When Jesus's family was violently forced to flee to Egypt during Herod's reign, they stood with those throughout world history who have been violently forced to leave their homeland (Matt. 2:13–23). When Jesus experienced political violence while being falsely incarcerated, he stood with the many people across history who have been unjustly imprisoned (Luke 22:47–52). When Jesus was chased by violent mobs, he stood in unity with the many who have been violently chased out of their families, workplaces, and countries (4:28–30). When Jesus experienced the personal violence of being stripped and beaten, he stood in solidarity with the many survivors of physical and sexual assault (John 19:1). Serene Jones writes, "Christ is the one who in the moment of crucifixion shows us that even in the depths of traumatic violence, God stands in solidarity with us."[18] One important result of engaging in nonviolent activism is that we express our solidarity with others who have suffered unjustly. Jesus extends nonviolent salvific solidarity toward us on the cross, and we are meant to go into the world and do the same.

Cross-Shaped Activism Sparks the Imagination

Cross-shaped activists are meant to see the cross as inspiration when devising plans to change the world. It is from the creativity of God that the Holy Spirit will grant us a holy imagination in a violent world. The cross was a tool reserved for political insurgents and treasonous peasants. It was a tool of intimidation and political power meant to strike fear in anyone who sought to stand up to the peace of Rome. The cross was the brute force of the firing squad, the electric chair, and the noose. It was meant to shame anyone associated with the one being crucified. The cross was a sinister invention of the sword. Yet, in God's infinite wisdom, the cross has

　　　　　　　　　　　　　　　　　　Practices of Justice

In God's infinite wisdom,
the cross has become
an everlasting emblem
of nonviolent creativity.

become an everlasting emblem of nonviolent creativity. From the cross comes eternal life, salvation from sins, rebirth into a global movement of Christians, and an imaginative spark everyday activists can rally around. If God can bring eternal Jubilee through the greatest emblem of violence in the first century, then the followers of Jesus can harness God's creative spirit to nonviolently work toward justice in the twenty-first century.[19] The question before the everyday activist is this: Will the church imagine how guns and swords can become objects and symbols of healing and cultivation?[20]

Everyday Activist
TAKEAWAYS

1 *Everyday activists embrace the cross as the model for Christian living.*

The cross teaches us to be humble, sacrificial, and willing to endure wrong. It shows us that we must refuse violence as the means of accomplishing peace. The cross has implications for our social life, our political life, our work life, and our family life. It shapes our very purpose as humans.[21] What does it look like for you to model this in your own life? The five principles of cross-shaped activism are a great place to begin thinking through how the cross can impact your everyday activism.

2 *Everyday activists identify how violence has infiltrated their understanding of discipleship and activism.*

God calls us to be like Matthew and reject the structural violence we are engaged in. God calls us to be like Simon the Zealot and abandon violence toward the state. God calls us, like he called James and John, not to respond to evil people with violent force. How have you allowed violent modes of discipleship to creep into your life? When have you justified domineering and coercing people? We must confront our own relationship with violence in order to repent, ask God for forgiveness, and begin working toward cross-shaped activism. The hard work starts with us!

3 *Everyday activists commit themselves to stand up to violence in the relationships that surround them.*

It is critical that you identify those who suffer from violence so you can stand up and call out this sin. In the United States, one in three women and one in four men experience violence from an intimate partner. Roughly twenty thousand calls per day are placed to the domestic violence hotline. One in five women will be raped in her lifetime.[22] Thousands of kids are violently abused every day without any recourse or reporting. It is incumbent upon everyday activists to do everything in their power to stand up to abusers, break the cycles of violence in our families, and embrace a cross-shaped way of living. This means refusing to fall into sinful patterns of violence ourselves while simultaneously resisting violence by standing up to those who are violent around us.[23]

FIGURE 9.1

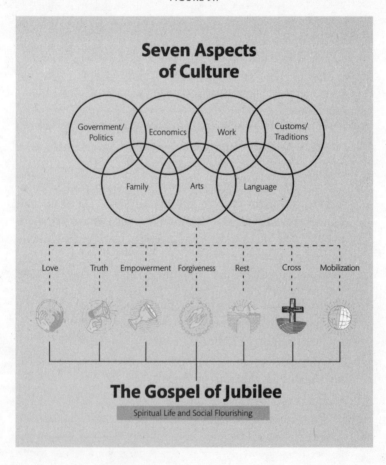

Practices of Justice

Reflection Questions

How does a culture of violence, force, and coercion impact your everyday life?

How can you apply the five principles of cross-shaped activism to have an impact on culture?

In what way is God calling you to personally reject violence in your own life, thoughts, and actions?

The church is called by God to be a sign of hope in the midst of despair, a place of healing in the depth of brokenness, and a guide in times of disorientation.

SAFWAT MARZOUK

Jesus' redeeming love draws us to God and turns us outward to the world with the face of the church. The church then proclaims a gospel that addresses both personal and systemic unraveling.

JOSÉ HUMPHREYS

Chapter Ten

Mobilization > Isolation

Main Thought

Everyday activists are called to mobilize in churches to create a just world.

Gospel Connect

Jesus died and rose again to bring us into a world-changing community.

Definitions

Church: Followers of Jesus on mission together

Mobilization: Gathering to proclaim and embody the gospel of Jubilee

Isolation: Following Jesus alone

Passages to Read

Matthew 28:18–20; Luke 4:14–21; 5:1–11; 6:12–16; 9:1–6; 10:1–2

So far, we have learned that fighting for justice is central to the ministry of Jesus. In Luke 4:16–21, Jesus declares the gospel of Jubilee—signaling that his message of salvation will bring both spiritual life and social flourishing. These two aspects of Jubilee are woven together throughout the ministry of Jesus, and some of the very best examples of them come from the early church. After God raised Jesus from the dead, men and women began to gather across the Roman Empire to declare that Jesus was alive. Much of the New Testament was written in this very context. The foundational truth that the Messiah had risen laid the groundwork for a movement that grew larger than anyone could have imagined. Churches popped up everywhere. These new Christians met in Jewish places of worship until they were kicked out. Then they met in people's homes. These early Christians embodied the very message of Luke 4:16–21—proclaiming liberty to prisoners, healing the sick, and helping people see their need to repent. It comes as no surprise, then, that many of the earliest Christians were from the margins of society. They were poor. They didn't have many resources. They were not famous. They didn't own lots of property. They gravitated toward the gospel of Jubilee, which offered forgiveness of sins and a community of Christians who were fierce advocates of justice and mercy.

One story in particular highlights the everyday activism that the early church displayed. This story contains one component that is central to everyday activism: mobilizing together for the work of justice. In the year 165, a deadly epidemic swept through the Roman Empire. While we are unsure about the specific disease, it was very contagious and had a high mortality rate. It lasted fifteen years! During those years, roughly three out of five people in the entire

Roman population died. Hundreds of thousands of bodies were carted out of city streets and public squares to be burned or buried. There was so much fear. There was no cure, and doctors couldn't do much for those suffering. When people displayed symptoms, they were often cast out by their family or thrown into the streets. One hundred years later, in 251, a second plague hit. Called the Plague of Cyprian, it is thought to have been an early form of smallpox. Around five thousand people died daily. This plague lasted roughly twenty years, killing millions of people. How did Christians respond in these times of massive social crisis? They engaged the crisis with acts of mercy and justice. Bishop Dionysius of Alexandria wrote a pastoral letter to Christians who gave their lives for the cause of Christian activism during the second plague:

> *Most of our brothers showed unbounded love and loyalty, never sparing themselves and thinking only of one another. Heedless of danger, they took charge of the sick, attending to their every need and ministering to them in Christ, and with them departed this life serenely happy; for they were infected by others with the disease, drawing on themselves the sickness of their neighbors and cheerfully accepting their pains. Many, in nursing and curing others, transferred their death to themselves and died in their stead. . . . The best of our brothers lost their lives in this manner, a number of presbyters, deacons, and laymen winning high commendation so that death in this form, the result of great piety and strong faith, seems in every way the equal to martyrdom.*[1]

This quotation shows how the early church mobilized to do the work of justice in the world. Did you catch what was said about piety? This early church pastor considered the acts of justice and mercy as reverent in nature. Bishop Dionysius saw the church's works of justice as holy. Christians did these acts of justice at great personal cost. Instead of falling into fear and caring only for their loved ones, Christians actively cared for those who were dying. They saw their faith as connected to the treatment of those who were suffering a painful death. One sociologist of religion notes that "what went on during the epidemics was only an intensification of what went on every day among Christians."[2] These early Christians show us thousands of years later how to boldly and fearlessly handle a pandemic![3] As African American theologian M. Shawn Copeland says, "Love of neighbor was the hallmark of early Christianity."[4]

There are lessons buried deep within the witness of the early church. What can we learn in the twenty-first century? The early church performed acts of justice together. Christians were committed to local churches. They didn't seek justice as individuals in isolation from the body of Christ. Christians came together to be God's people. They went out together to share God's love with those suffering. They ate together, prayed together, learned together, and shared their resources with each other (Acts 2:42–47).

While such acts may seem obvious for Christians to do, followers of Jesus have begun to drift away from church gatherings, many churches are on the decline, and Sunday services are becoming more optional. In the twenty-first century in the Western world, many have begun to drift away from local church engagement.[5] Maybe you are a part of a local church. Perhaps you have been hurt by a church. Some of you might be in leadership at a church. Others of you might not be going to a church at all.

To be fair, there are many reasons to stay away from churches. Churches often have bad leaders who abuse their power. Some are more like a social club. Some completely ignore the culture around them and become irrelevant. Others try to be so much like the culture that they simply mimic the latest cultural fads. Some churches are caught up in theological beliefs that are not important and teach the Bible in very inaccessible ways. Some churches are politically partisan. Others are all about big numbers, big budgets, and powerful male leaders. Some churches care only about how many souls they can win, while other congregations care only about social justice. There is no shortage of reasons to stay away from church.

Practices of Justice

The early church performed acts of justice together.

The truth is that many of these same problems existed in the early church. In fact, the early church was plagued with problems. I mean . . . really bad problems. There were church splits, church takeovers, infighting, confusion over the finances, leadership disagreements, overpowering leaders, people getting killed, sexual perversion, people getting banned from church, bad teaching, stolen money, public arguments, and gluttony. Yet, there has never been a time in the history of the Jesus movement when God's people have completely given up on the church. Why?

Jesus wants us in community.
Jesus wants us to gather together.
Jesus wants us to mobilize.

Jesus died to start the church.
Jesus resurrected to sustain the church.
Jesus is coming back to vindicate the church.

You are the church.
I am the church.

And together—we are the radical witness of Jesus on earth.

While we can debate what constitutes a church, or what a gathering should look like, or what types of churches we should attend, we can't get past the clear and present teachings of Jesus that we engage in the work of justice in the world through the community he died to start and rose again to sustain.

We can't be an everyday activist and ignore Jesus's radical practice of togetherness. Jesus died to bring us together and lived to show us how to be united. When Jesus could have given up on us, he stuck with this movement. Mobilizing together with other believers is a radical practice that should be embraced by anyone looking to engage in the work of justice in the world. In what follows, we will walk through some Gospel texts that show the growth of Jesus's movement.

Mobilizing as a Movement

When Jesus was born, Israel understood that the purposes of God in the world would be fulfilled through a specific community of people. The thought of following God outside of community was inconceivable. All throughout the Old Testament, God created various circles of community in order to accomplish the mission of God in the world. There were no solo heroes or lone wolves. There was no cowboy spirituality or "go at it yourself" justice work. While the Old Testament does contain stories of individuals, the individuals were always connected to a community they were working with, calling out, depending on, or partnering with. Let's look at a number of passages that show us how Jesus built an organized movement to radically change the world.

Jesus Starts the Movement (Luke 4:14–21)

When Jesus started his public ministry, he declared the gospel of Jubilee in a public forum: "The Spirit of the Lord is upon me, because he has anointed me to bring good news to the poor. He has sent me to proclaim release to the captives and recovery of sight to the blind, to let the oppressed go free, to proclaim the year of the Lord's favor" (Luke 4:18–19). Jesus announced that he had arrived, he was the Messiah, and he had come to bring the gospel of social flourishing and spiritual life to the world. After performing some miracles and preaching, Jesus entered the second stage of the movement. He gathered his disciples.

Jesus Calls the Twelve (Luke 5:1–11; 6:12–16; 9:1–6)

In Luke 5:1–11, Jesus calls Peter, James, and John while they are fishing. These guys worked long hours and didn't make much money. They were overtaxed and lived under the oppressive weight of the

Roman Empire. While it would have been normal for a rabbi like Jesus to teach them about religious matters, it was a radical step to stop working to follow Jesus. A short time later, Jesus formalizes the roster for the twelve disciples (Luke 6:12–16). In Luke 6:13, Jesus calls his followers "apostles." The term *apostle* means "one who is sent." Being apostles means that Jesus is sending the twelve as authorized agents of change in the world. The title gives them a collective meaning and purpose that Jesus has yet to fully explain. In Luke 9:1–6, Jesus sends his disciples out to proclaim the kingdom of God and heal those in need. Jesus gives them power and authority to execute the mission on his behalf.

The gathering and the naming of the twelve apostles teach us a few things. First, gathering the twelve disciples shows us that Jesus is not going to start his revolution alone. Jesus depends on the twelve, and the twelve depend on him. Community matters. Gathering people is necessary. The work of Jesus is not going to be done alone.

What can we learn from this?

When you dedicate your life to Christ,
you are brought into a community.

When God calls you to the work of justice,
he calls you to a movement of people.

When you decide to follow Jesus,
he walks you to his church and asks you to stay.

Second, when Jesus calls and names this small group of followers, he is performing an act of empowerment. Jesus immediately gives away his power and authority for the sake of the mission. He entrusts the message, the acts of compassion, the works of justice, and his movement into the hands of twelve ordinary people. These men are untested and unproven. Yet, Jesus gives them the keys to the kingdom (Matt. 16:17–20). Jesus does this to make the movement great. From this, we learn that everyday activists must actively give away power and entrust others with authority. Remember, it is hard to empower those around you if you are not around people! Jesus teaches us in the calling and naming of the twelve that it is vital to be in community and to empower those around us.

Jesus Gathers and Sends the Seventy-Two (Luke 10:1–2)

Soon after sending out the disciples, Jesus gathers more followers to take part in the work of the gospel. In Luke 10:1–2, we learn that the disciples increase in number from twelve to seventy-two:

> After this the Lord appointed seventy [seventy-two in some ancient authorities] others and sent them on ahead of him in pairs to every town and place where he himself intended to go. He said to them, "The harvest is plentiful, but the laborers are few; therefore ask the Lord of the harvest to send out laborers into his harvest."

These verses show the rapid growth of the movement. They show that Jesus wants people to prepare each town to meet him. It is remarkable how fast Jesus entrusts people to take the message and run with it. Even as the movement grows, however, the mission is meant to be done together. We learn from these verses that acts of mercy and justice are meant to be done in community. Even though we can't always be with Christians while at work, at school, or with family, we can have community with Christians at other touch points of the week. We simply can't follow Jesus alone and should therefore be looking for opportunities to gather with others to spread God's love and mercy in a hurting world. Put bluntly, we can't reject church.

Jesus Gives the Great Commission (Matthew 28:18–20)

Matthew 28 was written after Jesus died and was resurrected. After the women find the empty tomb, many begin to believe that Jesus is alive. Then Jesus begins appearing to the disciples and many others. Near the end of Jesus's time on earth, he gathers his disciples together to give them a commission. When Jesus called the twelve, he gave them authority. When he called the seventy-two, he gave them authority. When Jesus commissions his followers, he gives them authority with a specific set of instructions. These instructions apply to you and me this very day.

> And Jesus came and said to them, "All authority in heaven and on earth has been given to me. Go therefore and make disciples of all nations, baptizing them in the name of the Father and of the Son and of the Holy Spirit, and teaching them to obey everything that I have commanded you. And remember, I am with you always, to the end of the age." (Matt. 28:18–20)

These verses are pivotal for those who follow Jesus. We are called to help people follow Jesus wherever we find ourselves in the world. For the Jewish disciples, this meant that some of them would be leaving their homeland to serve in places around the world. For others, it meant serving Jesus where they were. Jesus says in verse 19 that we should baptize people in the name of God the Father, God the Son, and God the Holy Spirit. We must teach people to obey all Jesus's teachings.

These verses bring us full circle. To become a Christian is to accept the Luke 4:16–21 gospel of Jubilee. To follow Jesus is to enter his community and mobilize for the mission of God on earth. Jesus clarifies what this looks like practically in the Great Commission. People are saved. People are healed. People experience God's love and protection. People join the movement. People are baptized into a new identity as Jubilee creators. They are baptized into a new community that embodies God's Jubilee in community. Christians mobilize to change the world—wherever they are found on earth. We are called to be together in this mission of Jubilee. On the role of the church in the world, Dietrich Bonhoeffer wrote, "The church is the church only when it exists for others. The church must share in the secular problems of ordinary human life, not dominating, but helping and serving."[6] This important reflection hits on the very nature and meaning of the church. Through the church, we must address the ordinary situations of life and help through acts of justice.

We are called to be like the early church. Fearless. Radical. Active. The early Christians considered it their duty as followers of Jesus to share the gospel of Jubilee in word and deed. Their faith was active. They cared for those who suffered around them, not because they were perfect, their church was without fault, or they had it all together. Rather, they loved their neighbors in application of the Great Commission. They did it together. They mobilized together to bring about the work of God in the world.[7]

In the midst of global fears, international pandemics, postmodern anxieties, personal failures, church problems, and our daily pain, we must mobilize as the church.

I end with a reflection from Roberto Chao Romero. In his book *Brown Church*, he talks about his personal commitment, as a Mexican American Christian academic and activist, to the local church:

> I pursue justice and the Beloved Community in spiritual communion with the local church and the global body of Christ. Together with the apostle Paul, I recognize that I cannot long be a follower of Jesus outside of the church because, by God's design, we need one another, and belong to each other (1 Cor. 12:18–21; Rom. 12:5).[8]

The commitment to justice within the local church is a mark of Christian maturity. It is within this community that we have the confidence, love, and courage to enter our everyday as activists of our Lord.

The commitment
to justice within the
local church is a mark
of Christian maturity.

Everyday Activist
TAKEAWAYS

1 *Everyday activists identify a community of Christians to mobilize with.*

It is critical to find a local church where you can practice everyday activism. Who can you meet up with? Who can you pray with? Who can you learn from? Who can you teach? What pastors and leaders are worth following? Keep in mind that no church is perfect. No church is going to do everything right. No leader will have it all together. Churches are a reflection of our brokenness as humans. Yet, we can't give up on the local church. To love Jesus is to find a community and commit!

2 *Everyday activists find their role in the local church for the sake of the world.*

Once you commit yourself to a local community of Christians, look to get involved. Identify the works of justice and mercy that the church is doing. Find the leaders and ask them questions. Root yourself in the work that is already underway. Explore how your spiritual gifts connect to the needs of the church and the work of justice in the community. Find the path toward Christian maturity as you seek the welfare of the neighborhood. To love Jesus is to get involved in the community!

3 *Everyday activists are the change they want to see in the church.*

Oftentimes, a church doesn't have the outreach, justice focus, or mercy ministries that we wish it did. Perhaps the church spends too much money on things we don't think matter or is ignoring an injustice down the street. In these cases, I encourage you to do two things. First, go to the leadership with humility to express your desire to see the church engage in the areas of justice you care about. The hard truth is that more often than not you won't have the power or the church won't have the energy to engage in this justice work. So second, you should become the change in the church you want to see. Get engaged with the Christians from the church community who have similar passions. Link up and get to work, allowing your justice ministry to be a radical undercurrent of mercy in the church.

FIGURE 10.1

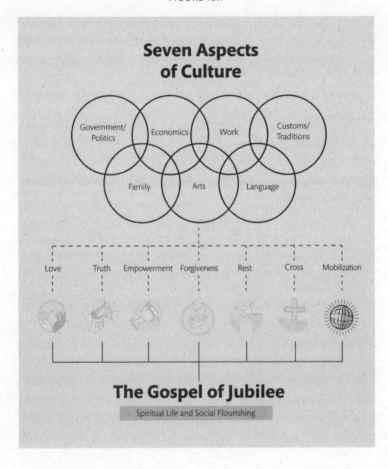

Reflection Questions

What local community of Christians has God called you to?

In what ways is God calling you to mobilize within the local church?

What are some local churches and organizations that are already mobilizing well?

A church that doesn't provoke any crises, a gospel that doesn't unsettle, a word of God that doesn't get under anyone's skin, a word of God that doesn't touch the real sin of the society in which it is being proclaimed—what gospel is that? The gospel is courageous; it's the good news of him who came to take away the world's sins.

OSCAR ROMERO

Jesus of Nazareth in his person embodies God's love and justice for the world. His teaching of the kingdom of God unveils the pretense of imperial power and offers the contours of a new order of love and justice.

ALEXIA SALVATIERRA and PETER HELTZEL

Conclusion

No matter who you are, where you are located, or what your day entails, you can make a difference in the world. While changing the world seems daunting, the blueprint has been provided by Jesus, and it is our responsibility to follow his way of life and his teachings and to spread the message of God's good Jubilee in a hurting world. The life of Jesus provides a path for everyday activism so we can make a difference in the various aspects of culture around us. Christian discipleship entails working alongside God to create a just world. We do this one day at a time, one social interaction at a time, and one loving gesture at a time. We do this by treating everyone as an image bearer of our great God and refusing to dehumanize people in the process of promoting justice.

In the first chapter, I defined culture as values, stories, and expressions that humans organize around. We looked at the seven components of culture that humans participate in. They are government/politics, economics, work, customs/traditions, family, arts, and language. These seven aspects of culture deeply affect our daily lives, our community experience, and the world around us. Humans reflect the image of God in the world by creating culture in these seven ways. Humans have the right to dignity and respect by virtue of the imago Dei. Yet, sin has corrupted the world. We see the way sinful humans can easily create unjust cultural systems when they abandon the call to reflect God's justice and goodness in the world. Jesus came to restore humans and the cosmos to God. The work of the church in the world is to take part in this restoration project.

In chapter 2, we learned how the gospel that Jesus proclaimed in Luke 4:16–21 is rooted in the Old Testament Year of Jubilee from Leviticus 25 and Isaiah 61. The gospel of Jubilee brings spiritual life and social flourishing for those who are suffering in every aspect of culture. Chinese American scholar Diane G. Chen writes that in

FIGURE 11.1

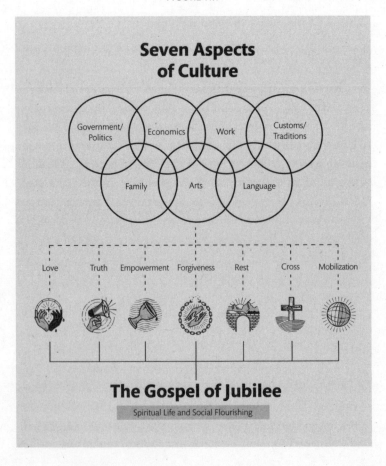

Seven Aspects of Culture

Government/Politics · Economics · Work · Customs/Traditions

Family · Arts · Language

Love · Truth · Empowerment · Forgiveness · Rest · Cross · Mobilization

The Gospel of Jubilee

Spiritual Life and Social Flourishing

Luke 4 "Jesus is making a bold claim that the salvation hoped for by generations of Israelites has arrived and he is the Spirit-anointed agent through whom all forms of oppression will be lifted."[1] Jesus's ministry to fight against all forms of social and spiritual oppression has been passed to us. African American pastor Eric Mason sums this up nicely by saying, "Jesus invites us to look at all of Scripture through the lens of justice."[2] The gospel of Jubilee is the foundation for everyday acts of justice and mercy.

In the ensuing chapters, we looked at seven radical practices of Jesus that Christians can adopt and apply on a daily basis. Figure 11.1 shows how these concepts come together. The foundation for all cultural change is the gospel of Jubilee. The spiritual life that God offers through Jesus activates the hearts of people to be different in the world.

In chapter 3, we learned that it is possible to create social change. When we apply the seven radical practices of Jesus in our everyday lives, we infuse love, truth, empowerment, forgiveness, rest, the cross, and mobilization into the culture around us. When we do this over time and with others, we have the capacity to create a just world. After looking at the latest research on social change, we discussed five steps for creating cultural change in everyday life.

Five Steps for Creating Cultural Change		
1.	Determination	You are noticeably convinced of neighbor love.
2.	Demonstration	You engage in neighbor love on a regular basis.
3.	Transmission	You practice neighbor love in situations where people notice and experience the benefit.
4.	Recruitment	You communicate to others why neighbor love will create a better culture.
5.	Mobilization	You practice neighbor love with others.

When we harness the power of the gospel, apply the teachings of Jesus in our everyday lives, and work alongside those who want to see the same change happen in our social and spiritual environments, the world can be changed. We can do it together. The world was meant to flourish. Our relationships were meant to thrive. Our communities were meant to be in right relationship with God. This is possible when we band together as everyday activists to make a difference.

Five Principles to Stay in the Fight

I want to leave you with five principles that will help you stay in the fight for justice when things get hard. Consider these principles a light to guide your way. These five principles are meant to guide you along the journey of Christian activism. Life is hard. Activism is difficult. One step forward in the fight is often followed by three steps backward. There is always more work than people. We must be able to sustain ourselves in the fight for justice. Take these principles as you go into the world to fight for God's Jubilee for all.

Principle #1: Stay in Relationship with Jesus

At the end of the day, all our activism efforts must connect back to our friendship and relationship with Jesus. Oftentimes, we do the work of justice on a foundation other than Jesus. Perhaps we do the work because we care so much about justice or we care so much about a specific issue. Perhaps we do the work because we hate injustice or we think we are better than other people. Perhaps we are acting out of personal guilt and remorse over past mistakes. Or perhaps we are responding to facts and statistics. We must reject all these faulty foundations for a real and present relationship with Jesus—the one who died on the cross to bring us into relationship with him. When we drift toward other motivations as the reason for our activism, we abandon the unending source of love, mercy, and justice. When you are having bad days of activism, run to Jesus. When you are having good days of activism, run to Jesus. When you need to get away to rest, do it with your Savior. The work of justice is not righting wrongs but honoring Jesus and sharing the power of

The fire of Christian activism is sustained only through a love for and a relationship with Jesus.

God's love. The fire of Christian activism is sustained only through a love for and a relationship with Jesus.

We engage in the work of justice in relationship with Jesus.

Principle #2: Be Motivated by Love

Everyday activists must be motivated by love. Many emotions and feelings can cause us to engage in an area of activism. We can be motivated by anger, rage, sadness, indifference, or compassion. Paul teaches us that when doing the work of God, love needs to be at the center of everything we do. In fact, we learn from 1 Corinthians 13 that we gain nothing and are nothing when we engage in the work of God without love! What are you most in love with? What about the work of justice do you love the most? We learn from Jesus that we must be in love with those who are suffering, in love with seeing the gospel of Jubilee expand gently into all creation, and in love with our Savior, who makes this all possible. Jesus reminds us that love of God and love of neighbor are paramount in the movement of God. When we replace our love of God and neighbor with love of justice, we replace God with an idol. We must keep the main thing the main thing.

We engage in the work of justice in relationship with Jesus while being motivated by love.

Principle #3: Rely on the Holy Spirit

The third principle we must follow is to rely on God the Holy Spirit. Jesus started his ministry only after the Holy Spirit came upon him. Real power rests in the work of the Holy Spirit living and breathing among his people. This is why we pray. This is why we remain fully reliant on God the Holy Spirit in the work of activism. We must petition the Holy Spirit in prayer to help us change the world in partnership with Jesus. We need strength from the Holy Spirit. We need comfort from the Holy Spirit. We need power from the Holy Spirit. We need courage from the Holy Spirit. We need wisdom that flows to us through the Holy Spirit. God's guarantee of a better world in the Holy Spirit was deposited into our hearts to bring lasting change to our lives, communities, and world. We must follow Jesus into reliance on the Holy Spirit. To do this is to rely on Jesus's plan.

We engage in the work of justice in relationship with Jesus while being motivated by love and relying on the Holy Spirit.

Principle #4: Stay Rooted in Scripture

While engaged in the work of justice, we must constantly root our vision of justice in the sacred text of Scripture. Moses, Ruth, Amos, Isaiah, Mary, and Martha are some of the people we can look to in the work of justice. We must find our place in the Scriptures, find our calling in the Scriptures, find our story in the Scriptures, and find our appeals to justice in the very life of Jesus. In the current historical moment, our culture's values and morals will come and go, shift and waver, rise and fall. While the scales of justice are always being moved based on the push and pull of the cultural moment, the doctrine of the imago Dei is fixed for all time. The practices of Jesus have been poured into the foundation of creation. The need for Jesus and the gospel of Jubilee is a fixed truth for all time. The shifting sand of our cultural moment is no match for the wisdom, mystery, and beauty found in the Scriptures.

We must always be looking to Jesus to justify our activism. We must always be looking to the ministry of Christ for our tactics, our methods, our motivations, and our mobilization strategies. While understanding the Scriptures can be difficult, we must press into the text in order to find the liberation humanity is longing for—the gospel of Jubilee.

We engage in the work of justice in relationship with Jesus while being motivated by love, relying on the Holy Spirit, and being rooted in Scripture.

Principle #5: Keep Faithfulness as the Aim

Finally, we engage in the work of justice in order to be faithful to Jesus and the gospel of Jubilee. While I have laid out a case for social change in this book, oftentimes God does not move the way we want. Other times culture does not change fast enough and it seems like unjust systems keep chugging along no matter how much we pray or work against evil. This can cause us to grow weary. Let me unburden you with a foundational principle: we worship Jesus through our everyday activism because it is the right thing to do, not because we are making progress. The cause of justice is worthy in and of itself because Jesus is worthy. Jesus values our contribution to the flourishing of the world regardless of the outcome. What a beautiful and freeing truth! There is intrinsic value in doing the right thing for Jesus. We can't place value just on the outcomes. Rather, we must measure our success by our ongoing faithfulness to the work God has called us to do.

We engage in the seven radical practices of Jesus not because it is easy, we will win, or we are guaranteed to change the world. Rather, we do it for Jesus. We do it in spite of the results because we want to worship and honor Jesus.

We engage in the work of justice in relationship with Jesus while being motivated by love, relying on the Holy Spirit, and being rooted in Scripture. We act to change the world alongside Jesus because we want to be faithful to his cause and call—not because we see change.

I end this book with an important quotation from Puerto Rican theologian Elizabeth Conde-Frazier, who speaks to this final principle:

A spiritual practice is carried out, therefore, not because it works but because it is good. It is a way of connecting with God, our neighbors, and our environment. The outcome of the practice is beyond us, but it is something we do together consistently. In this way, we help one another grow. We learn the practices in small increments of daily faithfulness.[3]

It is upon this daily faithfulness that we build our hope that the world can change, our communities can change, our hearts can be transformed for the sake of Jesus. We do the work of justice because it is the call of everyone who has been made in the image of God. We engage in everyday activism because we are called to spread and embody the gospel of Jubilee in a hurting world. We work together to see the seven aspects of culture change so more people can flourish. We work to restore our neighborhoods and all creation because Jesus came to earth, died, and resurrected to new life. This is what it means to be an everyday activist.

Reflection Questions

Which of the seven practices in this book is God calling you to focus on?

Which of the seven areas of culture should you be focused on changing?

How can you daily embody the gospel of Jubilee in your local setting?

Final Benediction

King of all justice,

Help us become everyday activists—
faithful to your gospel of Jubilee
and more in love with your Son.

Fill us with your justice and mercy
until your Jubilee is known by everyone.

Amen.

Appendix 1

Justice Matrix

Purpose

This appendix is dedicated to helping you think through the specific areas of justice you want to engage in.

When considering getting involved in the work of justice, it can be overwhelming figuring out where to start. There are literally thousands of wonderful justice-focused organizations, community projects, and local initiatives in which to get involved.

When Christians start talking about justice, we often end up speaking right past each other. Some people care so much about a particular issue that it can seem like they do not care about other important problems. Some care so much about fighting injustice through fostering kids that they might not have the emotional space to think through the global refugee crisis. Some Christians feel called to national politics, while others may focus on the good work being done on a local political level. Here is what you need to know: it is important for you to focus your efforts where you can make a long-lasting difference. This means that you won't be able to pursue every cause you care about. That's okay! You are one person. The challenge in the digital age is tempering our focus on the things that are before us.

The justice matrix is a tool to help you think through the areas of justice you can engage in. The bottom horizontal section of the justice matrix is called strategies of Jubilee. This section has three boxes titled prevention, intervention, and reclamation. The horizontal part of the justice matrix is called geography of Jubilee. This section has three boxes called local/regional, national, and international. I briefly describe each section and give some examples for each box. At the end, I provide space for you to fill out your own justice matrix to determine the areas you plan to engage in.

Strategies of Jubilee

If the overall goal is creating a just world, a strategy is a specific plan to achieve the goal. There are three basic strategies of Jubilee that can be deployed within a local church, a group of churches, a nonprofit, or even a for-profit business. In this section, I use a local neighborhood in Los Angeles called Highland Park to illustrate what these three strategies can look like.

It is important to note that these three strategies are not isolated from each other, nor do they exclude each other. The point of breaking these into three separate areas is to help the everyday activist think through the area they want to engage in, identify the issues that face their own community, and measure the potential impact they can have. The more you dive into the work of justice in the world, the more you discover how these lines blur in your own life and in the lives of those God has called you to love.

Prevention

Prevention is when a person, group of people, or formal organization serves individuals, families, or communities that are vulnerable to injustice. After-school programs are a great example of a prevention strategy to help kids stay off the street, connect with mentors, get homework done, socialize with other kids, and stay safe while parents are at work. The following are some examples of preventative causes that Christians can engage in:

- community sports/arts
- parent/guardian support
- environmental care

Intervention

Intervention is a program or process that serves individuals, families, or communities facing an immediate crisis. For example, a local nonprofit in the Highland Park neighborhood does gang intervention for families. When a teenager joins a local gang, the organization comes into the family to serve the younger brothers and sisters, offering them social support so they will not get caught up in the same gang activity. They offer a nonjudgmental approach to love and care for the kids within the family system. The following are some examples of intervention causes that Christians can engage in:

- social services
- foster care / adoption
- crisis counseling services
- urban tree planting

Reclamation

Reclamation is serving individuals, families, or communities that are looking to repair or reclaim something for the sake of human flourishing. In Highland Park, a number of churches started rehab programs for ex-convicts, ex-addicts, and young adults who are trying to get off the streets. The churches house, feed, and are a bridge between the spiritual needs and the social needs of these individuals who are trying to recover their lives. The following are some examples of rehabilitation causes that Christians can engage in:

- addiction rehab
- post-trauma support
- neighborhood revitalization

Geography of Jubilee

Geography of Jubilee refers to the geographic focus of your justice work: local/regional, national, and international. Each person made in God's image will feel a unique pull in one or more of these directions. Once you have these three areas of focus in mind, you will begin noticing various nonprofits or churches that focus on a particular geographical location.

Local/Regional

The first geographical area to consider is local and regional. This is your neighborhood, the town you live in, and the surrounding area. Each of these local areas has its own culture, needs, and specific injustices that an everyday activist can address. The following are some examples of local/regional issues of justice that Christians can engage in:

- supporting local businesses
- fighting gentrification
- homelessness support
- renter rights advocacy
- addressing food deserts

National

The second geographical area to consider is national. Whether you live in the United States or another nation, you will find issues that are unique to vulnerable populations on a continental scale. The following are some examples of national issues of justice that Christians can engage in:

- economic policy
- immigration policy
- workers' rights
- mass incarceration

International

The third geographical area to consider is international. People all over the world face certain issues on a regular basis. The following are some examples of international issues of justice that Christians can engage in:

- sex trafficking
- global warming
- refugee crisis
- natural disaster relief

Steps to Using the Matrix

1. Identify your areas of interest and passion that already intersect with your life.
2. Ask trusted friends, "What areas of passion do you see in my life?"
3. Identify how they might fit into the matrix.
4. Fill in the matrix.

Take a few minutes to consider my sample justice matrix (fig. A.1) on the next page. Then, once you understand the matrix, begin filling out your own (fig. A.2) with the areas in which you are already involved or want to be involved. Pay special attention to the ways in which the local areas impact the national and international areas and vice versa. Think about the ways that prevention, intervention, and reclamation overlap. And . . . go!

FIGURE A.1

Josh's Justice Matrix

Geography of Jubilee

	Prevention	Intervention	Reclamation
International			Sexual Survivor Support Freely in Hope (freelyinhope.org)
National		Support the Poor People's Campaign Starting Pax (madeforpax.org)	Support Raw Tools (rawtools.com)
Local/Regional	After-School Arts Local Church Involvement	Youth Mentoring Local Church Involvement	Local Church Involvement

Strategies of Jubilee

FIGURE A.2

Jubilee Action Plan

Purpose

This appendix is dedicated to helping you begin to develop an action plan.

If you are not sure where to get started, this action plan will help you think through what aspects of justice you should be engaging in. The plan is meant to help anyone who desires to engage in the work of justice but is not sure where to start. This can also be done in groups.

While I list five separate steps, think of them as overlapping circles. Don't look at this action plan as a static process to follow (though that might help some of you). Rather, move fluidly through the process as someone looking to spread Jubilee in the world. For instance, you might want to start with step 4, "Reflect with God," first. That is fine. Our lives, our minds, and our processes with Jesus aren't always super structured. That is okay. Let this be scaffolding for the activism God is building in your life.

Jubilee Action Plan

Step 1: Think Local to Identify Your Focus

Step 1 is to identify the area of focus you are called to. Look around at your community, your workplace, and your everyday life.

Regardless of the justice issue you are drawn to, it will most likely have a local manifestation. For instance, if you care about global warming, you can plant trees or sell your car. If you care about the refugee crisis, then identify a local community where refugees are resettling and ask what you can do to help. International and global issues become local really quick!

List three local areas of interest and circle the one you are most interested in:

Step 2: Learn All You Can

Step 2 involves learning all you can about the issue. Too often people jump from the "need" to the "solution." This is really dangerous. If you are looking to engage in an area of justice and you don't have any experience, become a learner first. Even if you have experience in a particular area of injustice (say you came from the foster care system), it is critical that you don't go into your work with all the answers and solutions. This is also dangerous. Read books, watch YouTube videos, and interview and follow people who are doing the work online and in real life. Don't do this once. Do it over and over again. Be curious. If you are not a learner, you will create harm in your work.

Do some research and then complete the lists below.

These are the five online sources I am going to follow:

These are the two books I am going to read:

These are the three people I am going to talk with to learn from:

Step 3: Find an Organization

After you have engaged in the learning process, step 3 is to find an organization that is already doing the work. This means you do *not* need to start something yourself. Trying to do an act of justice all by yourself is a bad next step. I suggest identifying a church or a nonprofit that is in your area or somewhere near you. Once you find a place that resonates with you, reach out and ask someone to meet for coffee or lunch so you can learn more. Before you do this, read everything on their website and find out as much as you can. Write down a list of questions. For example, "For someone in my situation, where is the best place to start?" and "What are the biggest lessons your organization has learned about engaging in this work?" and "What are the greatest areas of need in your organization?" Don't get discouraged! Many people won't want to meet with you. That is okay. Just keep asking until someone says yes. If necessary, show up in person and ask to talk to someone.

These are the three organizations I want to learn more about:

Step 4: Reflect with God

Step 4 is to reflect with God on what you have been learning. Pray and ask God to direct you. Talk to trusted friends. Look at the stories of Jesus in the Bible and ask God how you can become more like Jesus through your activism. Talk to your pastor. Pray about whether you should join a particular church or serve in a particular nonprofit. Look up passages that relate to the issue in focus. Can you find God's heart for this issue in the Bible? Where? What happened? This is a critical next step in your journey.

I will look at these passages in the Bible:

I will take reflection time at this location to speak to God and process:

Step 5: Act in Partnership

At step 5, you are ready to act in partnership with the church or organization that you desire to serve with locally. It is critical to see yourself as coming alongside what God is already doing and serving where God is already at work. You want to see yourself as a learner on the journey toward Jubilee. Partner as one who will not save people from injustice but will learn how to live Jubilee together. Leverage your time, privilege, and experience to serve with those who desire to partner in the work of justice.

There are three ways to act in partnership.

SHORT-TERM

First, you can serve in an area of justice through a one-time experience. While the impact will probably be smaller than that of the next two forms of action, the experience will serve to expose you to the work of justice that you think you are called into. You need to go out and picket before you become an organizer. You need to attend a renters' rights trial before creating a renters' rights workshop. It is critical to gain short-term experiences before diving too deep into an area of focus.

ONGOING

Second, you can serve on an ongoing basis in a church or organization. This could be giving your time to an internship, giving financially over time, or even getting a job serving in an area of justice you love. Once you have done one or two exposure projects, think about ways to get more involved. This might even mean taking a few college classes in your area and learning more about the ways you can involve yourself in the work of justice.

CAREER PATH

The last way to act is to follow a career path in which you become a thought leader, activist, or professional in an area of justice. You could become a public speaker, writer, lawyer, pastor, social worker, political scientist, politician, or cultivator of land. This option is for people who have already explored short-term experiences and have engaged in ongoing service in an area of justice. They feel called to do more, be more, and dive headlong into a legacy-building project of bringing the gospel of Jubilee into one area of creation.

Appendix 3

Life of Jesus Starter Kit

Purpose

This appendix is dedicated to helping you go deeper into the Scriptures.

If you read this book and wish I dove deeper into biblical interpretation, theological reflection, or cultural analysis of the verses and you want to know how you can learn for yourself what these passages mean, there are many ways you can continue to study the Scriptures. I encourage you to use the endnotes to identify the books and authors that pique your interest. If you are interested in focusing more on the life of Jesus and the surrounding sociocultural context that the New Testament was written in, here is a starter list of books and resources I found helpful in my research. Happy reading!

New Testament Introduction

deSilva, David A. *An Introduction to the New Testament: Context, Methods and Ministry Formation.* Downers Grove, IL: InterVarsity, 2018.

Hagner, Donald A. *The New Testament: A Theological and Historical Introduction.* Grand Rapids: Baker Academic, 2012.

New Testament—Historical Background

Burge, Gary M., and Gene L. Green. *The New Testament in Antiquity: A Survey of the New Testament within Its Cultural Context.* Grand Rapids: Zondervan, 2020.

Tenney, Merrill. *New Testament Times: Understanding the World of the First Century.* Grand Rapids: Baker Books, 2004.

Wright, N. T. *The New Testament and the People of God.* Minneapolis: Fortress, 1992.

New Testament—Cultural Background

Bailey, Kenneth E. *Jesus Through Middle Eastern Eyes: Cultural Studies in the Gospels.* Downers Grove, IL: InterVarsity, 2008.

Hanson, K. C., and Douglas E. Oakman. *Palestine in the Time of Jesus: Social Structures and Social Conflicts.* 2nd ed. Minneapolis: Fortress, 2008.

Porter, Stanley E., and Cynthia Long Westfall, eds. *Empire in the New Testament.* Eugene, OR: Wipf & Stock, 2011.

New Testament—Cultural Background (Verse by Verse)

Keener, Craig S. *The InterVarsity Press Bible Background Commentary: New Testament.* Downers Grove, IL: InterVarsity, 2014.

New Testament—Theology

Bauckham, Richard. *Jesus: A Very Short Introduction.* Oxford, UK: Oxford University Press, 2011.

Blomberg, Craig L. *A New Testament Theology.* Waco: Baylor, 2018.

Cone, James H. *The Cross and the Lynching Tree.* Maryknoll, NY: Orbis, 2013.

Ladd, George E. *A Theology of the New Testament.* Rev. ed. Edited by Donald A. Hagner. Grand Rapids: Eerdmans, 1993.

Levine, Amy-Jill. *The Misunderstood Jew: The Church and the Scandal of the Jewish Jesus.* New York: Harper, 2007.

Martinez-Olivieri, Jules A. *A Visible Witness: Christology, Liberation and Participation*. Minneapolis: Fortress, 2016.

Stuhlmacher, Peter. *Biblical Theology of the New Testament*. Grand Rapids: Eerdmans, 2018.

Four Gospels—Introduction

Blomberg, Craig L. *Jesus and the Gospels: An Introduction and Survey*. 2nd ed. Nashville: B&H Academic, 2009.

Powell, Mark Alan. *Fortress Introduction to the Gospels*. 2nd ed. Minneapolis: Fortress, 2019.

Strauss, Mark. *Four Portraits, One Jesus: A Survey of Jesus and the Gospels*. 2nd ed. Grand Rapids: Zondervan, 2020.

Four Gospels—Theology

Bauckham, Richard. *Jesus and the Eyewitnesses: The Gospels as Eyewitness Testimony*. Grand Rapids: Eerdmans, 2017.

Wright, N. T. *Jesus and the Victory of God*. Minneapolis: Fortress, 1996.

———. *The Resurrection of the Son of God*. Minneapolis: Fortress, 2003.

Jubilee

Bruno, Christopher R. "Jesus Is Our Jubilee . . . but How? The OT Background and Lukan Fulfillment of the Ethics of Jubilee." *Journal of the Evangelical Theological Society* 53, no. 1 (March 2010): 81–101.

Kinsler, Ross, and Gloria Kinsler. *The Biblical Jubilee and the Struggle for Life: An Invitation to Personal, Ecclesial, and Social Transformation*. Maryknoll, NY: Orbis, 1999.

Leiter, David A. "The Year of Jubilee and the 21st Century." *Brethren Life and Thought* 47, nos. 3–4 (2002): 164–86.

Miura, Nozomi. "Justice in the Bible, Globalization and Jubilee." *Journal of Theta Alpha Kappa* 28, no. 2 (2004): 38–57.

North, Robert. *The Biblical Jubilee: After Fifty Years*. Richardson, TX: Biblical Institute Press, 2002.

Ringe, Sharon H. *Jesus, Liberation, and the Biblical Jubilee: Images for Ethics and Christology*. Eugene, OR: Wipf & Stock, 1985.

Sanders, James A. "Jubilee in the Bible." *Biblical Theology Bulletin: Journal of Bible and Culture* 50, no. 1 (February 2020): 4–6.

Tan, Kim. *Jubilee and Social Justice: A Dangerous Quest to Overcome Inequalities*. Nashville: Abingdon, 2021.

Tiessen, Calvin. "Jubilee, Discipleship and Social Rest." *Transformation: An International Journal of Holistic Mission Studies* 36, no. 2 (April 2019): 113–26.

Wright, Christopher J. H. "Theology of Jubilee: Biblical, Social and Ethical Perspectives." *Evangelical Review of Theology* 41, no. 1 (2017): 6–30.

Notes

Introduction

1. If you want to see how these titles connect to the Gospels, I suggest Mark Strauss, *Four Portraits, One Jesus: A Survey of Jesus and the Gospels*, 2nd ed. (Grand Rapids: Zondervan, 2020).

2. Nicholas P. Wolterstorff, *Journey toward Justice: Personal Encounters in the Global South* (Grand Rapids: Baker Academic, 2013), 87.

Chapter 1 Creating a Just World

1. I'll be using the words *justice* and *righteousness* interchangeably in this book. The Hebrew and Greek words for justice/righteousness are often used interchangeably and mean the same thing. (1) I will therefore not make a major distinction between the two words. To be righteous is to be just. To be just is to be righteous. (2) I will assume that these words can refer to one's individual life before God or broader systems we interact with as humans. This holistic thinking best honors the culture and thinking of those who wrote the Bible. For a biblical basis, see Christopher Wright, *Old Testament Ethics for the People of God* (Downers Grove, IL: InterVarsity, 2004), chap. 8.

2. For more on the concept of the imago Dei, see John F. Kilner, *Dignity and Destiny: Humanity in the Image of God* (Grand Rapids: Eerdmans, 2015); and International Commission for Anglican-Orthodox Theological Dialogue, *In the Image and Likeness of God: A Hope-Filled Anthropology—The Buffalo Statement* (London: Anglican Communion Office, 2015).

3. Vincent E. Bacote, *The Political Disciple: A Theology of Public Life* (Grand Rapids: Zondervan, 2015), 41.

4. For more on this, see M. Daniel Carroll R., *The Bible and Borders: Hearing God's Word on Immigration* (Grand Rapids: Brazos, 2020), 9–15; and Nicholas P. Wolterstorff, *Journey toward Justice: Personal Encounters in the Global South* (Grand Rapids: Baker Academic, 2013), chaps. 6–11, 21.

5. Eloise Meneses, *Studying the Image: Critical Issues in Anthropology for Christians* (Eugene, OR: Cascade, 2019), loc. 760, Kindle.

6. Some scholars understand Genesis 1:26–28 to be the cultural mandate in which God calls humans to go into the world and create families, artwork, networks of people, commerce, cities, and governments that are both good and just. For more on this, see William Edgar, *Created and Creating: A Biblical Theology of Culture* (Downers Grove, IL: InterVarsity, 2016), chap. 8.

7. For an important discussion on how humans reflect God as cultural beings, see Michelle Ami Reyes, *Becoming All Things: How Small Changes Lead to Lasting Connections Across Cultures* (Grand Rapids: Zondervan, 2021), chap. 1.

8. Chris Marshall notes that there are four connected components of biblical justice. They are distribution, equity, power, and rights. Chris Marshall, *The Little Book of Biblical Justice: A Fresh Approach to the Bible's Teachings on Justice* (New York: Good Books, 2005).

9. Jessica Nicholas, *God Loves Justice: A User-Friendly Guide to Biblical Justice and Righteousness* (Los Angeles: S&E Educational, 2017), loc. 931, Kindle.

10. Craig G. Bartholomew and Michael W. Goheen, *The Drama of Scripture: Finding Our Place in the Biblical Story* (Grand Rapids: Baker Academic, 2014), 481–82.

11. For more biblical teaching on the concept of justice, see Timothy Keller, *Generous Justice: How God's Grace Makes Us Just* (New York: Penguin, 2012).

12. For the sake of the book, I'll keep the definition of culture very simple. To dive deeper, see Stephan A. Grunlan and Marvin K. Mayers, *Cultural Anthropology: A Christian Perspective*, 2nd ed. (Grand Rapids: Zondervan, 1988), 38–50; and Brian M. Howell and Jenell Paris, *Introducing Cultural Anthropology: A Christian Perspective* (Grand Rapids: Baker Academic, 2019), chap. 2. In this simple definition of culture, I'm accounting for culture as (1) narratives or stories and (2) what humans cultivate and build in the world. Different academic disciplines emphasize one over the other. Yet, we see both happening in the Bible. To learn more about the academic developments of historic particularism (emphasizing stories/narratives) or structural functionalism (emphasizing structures/systems), see Kenneth J. Guest, *Essentials of Cultural Anthropology: A Toolkit for a Global Age*, 3rd ed. (New York: Norton, 2020), chap. 2.

13. The remarkable fact is that you can look across every culture in the world and find these seven aspects of culture. The image of God bursts out of every large grouping of humans whether they know about Jesus or not. Humans can't help but reflect God through the creation of these cultural systems.

14. I am purposefully leaving out religion as an aspect of culture that humans organize around. For the sake of this book, the Christian faith or "religion" is the prism through which we should be understanding the rest of these cultural systems. For this reason, I won't place religion as equal to these other aspects of culture. To explore the place of religion in the study of culture and anthropology, see Rebecca Stein and Philip L. Stein, *The Anthropology of Religion, Magic, and Witchcraft*, 4th ed. (London: Routledge, 2017).

15. If you want a great resource on this theme from a BIPOC perspective, see Elsa Tamez, *Bible of the Oppressed* (Eugene, OR: Wipf & Stock, 2006).

16. Ivone Gebara, *Out of the Depths: Women's Experience of Evil and Salvation*, trans. Ann Patrick Ware (Minneapolis: Fortress, 2002), loc. 1556, Kindle.

Chapter 2 The Gospel of Jubilee

1. More specifically, the evangelical churches I grew up in adopted the Focus on the Family, Republican platform that picked and chose the justice issues that apply to the white, middle-class, nuclear family while ignoring other justice issues that affected communities of color. Moreover, the white conservative churches were highly individualist and unhealthily split the spiritual and the social into two separate categories.

2. Esteban Voth, "The Biblical Basis for Integral Mission in the Context of Poverty," in *The Local Church, Agent of Transformation: An Ecclesiology of Integral Mission*, ed. Tetsunao Yamamori and C. René Padilla (Buenos Aires: Kairos, 2004), 74.

3. One of the core methodological assumptions in this chapter is that we should understand all aspects of the gospel in light of Luke 4. While all metaphors and descriptions of the gospel are critically important, we would be remiss not to prioritize the words of Jesus when trying to understand the gospel. This means that we should understand the other facets of the gospel (justification by faith, adoption, being born again, being coheirs with Christ, etc.) in light of Jubilee, not the other way around.

4. To go deeper into the meaning of Luke 4 and the gospel of Jubilee, see Bryan R. Dyer, "Good News to the Poor: Social Upheaval, Strong Warnings and Sincere Giving in Luke-Acts," in *The Bible and Social Justice: Old Testament and New Testament Foundations for the Church's Urgent Call*, ed. Cynthia Long Westfall and Bryan R. Dyer (Eugene, OR: Wipf & Stock, 2016), 118–39; Joel B. Green, *The Theology of the Gospel of Luke* (Cambridge, UK: Cambridge University Press, 1995), 76–101; and André Trocmé, *Jesus and the Nonviolent Revolution* (Walden, NY: Plough, 2014).

5. For a deeper interpretation of and theological reflection on Leviticus 25, see Christopher Wright, *Old Testament Ethics for the People of God* (Downers Grove, IL: InterVarsity, 2004), 202–11.

6. Richard H. Lowery, *Sabbath and Jubilee* (St. Louis: Chalice Press, 2000), 146.

7. C. René Padilla, *Mission Between the Times: Essays on the Kingdom* (Carlisle, UK: Langham, 2013), 98.

8. Melba Padilla Maggay, *Transforming Society* (Eugene, OR: Wipf & Stock, 2011), 12.

9. Sharon H. Ringe, *Jesus, Liberation, and the Biblical Jubilee: Images for Ethics and Christology* (Eugene, OR: Wipf & Stock, 1985), 28.

10. Dyer, "Good News to the Poor," 121.

11. C. René Padilla notes that without a holistic vision of transformation, either the work of the church will fall into a private morality that does not touch the suffering of our world, or the church will be captured by popular ideologies that will use the Christian message to legitimize injustice. We can see this playing out in twenty-first-century America with the political left/right divides in the church. See C. René Padilla, "The Biblical Basis for Social Ethics," in *Transforming the World? The Gospel and Social Responsibility*, ed. Jamie A. Grant and Dewi A. Hughes (Nottingham, UK: Inter-Varsity, 2009), 187–204.

12. Dr. John Perkins calls the holistic gospel the "whole" gospel in John M. Perkins, *Let Justice Roll Down* (Grand Rapids: Baker Books, 2012). Lisa Sharon Harper calls the holistic gospel the "very good" gospel in Lisa Sharon Harper, *The Very Good Gospel: How Everything Wrong Can Be Made Right* (Colorado Springs: WaterBrook, 2016). Another great book to read that captures the holistic nature of

the gospel is Richard Stearns, *The Hole in Our Gospel: What Does God Expect of Us?* (Nashville: Thomas Nelson, 2009).

13. While the Year of Jubilee from Leviticus 25 is one way to thread God's spiritual life and social liberation through the story of the Bible, we see the liberative work begin in the exodus. When Jesus reveals himself as the I AM (John 8:58) and Scripture names Jesus the greater Moses (Deut. 18:15–19; Acts 7:37), we learn that a new social and spiritual exodus is manifesting in Jesus's ministry. For more on how the exodus story connects to Jesus and gives us a picture of economic, spiritual, social, political, and cultural restoration, see Christopher J. H. Wright, *The Mission of God's People: A Biblical Theology of the Church's Mission* (Grand Rapids: Zondervan, 2010), chap. 6.

14. To go deeper into this social/spiritual divide that the Western church has suffered from, see Bryant L. Myers, *Walking with the Poor: Principles and Practices of Transformational Development*, rev. ed. (Maryknoll, NY: Orbis, 2011), loc. 596–696, Kindle.

15. Ruth Padilla DeBorst, "Church, Power, and Transformation in Latin America: A Different Citizenship Is Possible," in *The Church from Every Tribe and Tongue: Ecclesiology in the Majority World*, eds. Gene L. Green, Stephen T. Pardue, and K. K. Yeo (Carlisle, UK: Langham Global Library, 2018), loc. 1188, Kindle.

16. Barbara A. Holmes, *Joy Unspeakable: Contemplative Practices of the Black Church* (Minneapolis: Fortress, 2017), 114.

Chapter 3 How Social Change Happens

1. Bethany Hanke Hoang and Kristen Deede Johnson, *The Justice Calling: Where Passion Meets Perseverance* (Grand Rapids: Brazos, 2017), 115.

2. Everett M. Rogers, *Diffusion of Innovations*, 5th ed. (New York: Free Press, 2003).

3. Shane Claiborne, *The Irresistible Revolution, Updated and Expanded: Living as an Ordinary Radical* (Grand Rapids: Zondervan, 2016), 321.

4. Damon Centola, *How Behavior Spreads: The Science of Complex Contagions* (Princeton: Princeton University Press, 2020), 173.

5. J. Xie, S. Sreenivasan, G. Korniss, W. Zhang, C. Lim, and B. K. Szymanski, "Social Consensus through the Influence of Committed Minorities," *Physical Review E* 84, no. 1 (July 2011): 1–9.

6. James K. A. Smith, *You Are What You Love: The Spiritual Power of Habit* (Grand Rapids: Brazos, 2016), 18.

7. For more on social change, see Matthew O. Jackson, *The Human Network: How Your Social Position Determines Your Power, Beliefs, and Behaviors* (New York: Pantheon, 2019); and Cass R. Sunstein, *How Change Happens* (Cambridge: MIT, 2020).

8. There are more types of social change, but for the sake of simplicity, I'll feature only three. If you want a more detailed overview, see Emmaline Soken-Huberty, "What Is Social Change?," Human Rights Careers, accessed December 10, 2021, https://www.humanrightscareers.com/issues/what-is-social-change/; and "Understanding Social Change," in *Sociology: Understanding and Changing the Social World* (Minneapolis: University of Minnesota Libraries Publishing, 2021), https://open.lib.umn.edu/sociology/chapter/20-1-understanding-social-change.

9. Keep in mind that more often than not, people in power will default to gradual change over the option of sudden change. They prefer releasing the social pressure of change through dialogue, listening, and making very small changes that they hope appease change agents.

Chapter 4 Love > Fear

1. For more on the topic of fear in light of following Jesus, see Howard Thurman, *Jesus and the Disinherited* (Boston: Beacon Press, 1996), chap. 2.

2. Howard Thurman, *Howard Thurman: Sermons on the Parables*, ed. David B. Gowler and Kipton E. Jensen (Maryknoll, NY: Orbis, 2018).

3. A good interpretation and application of this parable can be found in Timothy Keller, *Generous Justice: How God's Grace Makes Us Just* (New York: Penguin, 2012).

4. Nélida Ritchie, "Women and Christology," in *Through Her Eyes: Women's Theology from Latin America*, ed. Elsa Tamez (Eugene, OR: Wipf & Stock, 1989), 86.

5. Yolanda Pierce, *In My Grandmother's House: Black Women, Faith, and the Stories We Inherit* (Minneapolis: Broadleaf, 2021), 17.

6. Mark R. Glanville and Luke Glanville, *Refuge Reimagined: Biblical Kinship in Global Politics* (Downers Grove, IL: InterVarsity, 2021), 89.

7. Martin Luther King Jr., "I've Been to the Mountaintop," American Rhetoric: Top 100 Speeches, accessed January 12, 2022, https://www.americanrhetoric.com/speeches/mlkivebeentothemountaintop.htm.

8. A great reflection on the response of the church to embody neighbor love as an expression of the gospel can be found in Tim Chester, ed., *Justice, Mercy, and Humility: Integral Mission and the Poor* (Carlisle, UK: Paternoster, 2002), 102–11.

9. To explore the concept of neighbor love within the biblical concept of kinship, see Glanville and Glanville, *Refuge Reimagined*, 87–94.

Chapter 5 Truth > Lies

1. Oscar Romero, *The Violence of Love*, trans. James R. Brockman (Maryknoll, NY: Orbis, 2004), 115.

2. Romero, *Violence of Love*, 121.

3. Walter Brueggemann, *Truth Speaks to Power: The Countercultural Nature of Scripture* (Louisville: Westminster John Knox Press, 2013), 110.

4. Furthermore, many Christians from places of privilege are unaware how the prophetic tradition in the Old Testament connects to a Christian in their everyday life. While the prophetic tradition has been alive and thrived among African American, Latin American, and Asian American Christian communities, it has been discarded by many Christians of privilege. Why? It calls into question the wealth of the white church, it challenges the business-driven megachurch models of the Western church, and it calls to account white Christian complicity and complacency throughout American history.

5. Justin Giboney, Michael Wear, and Chris Butler, eds., *Compassion (&) Conviction: The AND Campaign's Guide to Faithful Civic Engagement* (Downers Grove, IL: InterVarsity, 2020).

6. Soong-Chan Rah, *The Next Evangelicalism: Freeing the Church from Western Cultural Captivity* (Downers Grove, IL: InterVarsity, 2009), loc. 905, Kindle.

7. If you are not sure about the claim that the United States was not founded as a Christian nation, see Gregory A. Boyd, *The Myth of a Christian Nation: How the Quest for Political Power Is Destroying the Church* (Grand Rapids: Zondervan, 2005); Mark Charles, *Unsettling Truths: The Ongoing Dehumanizing Legacy of the Doctrine of Discovery* (Downers Grove, IL: InterVarsity, 2019); John Fea, *Was America Founded as a Christian Nation? A Historical Introduction*, rev. ed. (Louisville: Westminster John Knox, 2016); and Edward J. Blum and Paul Harvey, *The Color of Christ: The Son of God and the Saga of Race in America* (Chapel Hill: University of North Carolina Press, 2012).

8. African theologian Emmanuel Katongole discusses how the church must foster "Prophetic Interruptions" amid political ideologies that end up harming our communities. In *Mirror to the Church*, Katongole uses the Rwandan genocide to illustrate the dangers of failing to develop a public witness to the truth of Jesus. See Emmanuel Katongole and Jonathan Wilson-Hartgrove, *Mirror to the Church: Resurrecting Faith after Genocide in Rwanda* (Grand Rapids: Zondervan, 2009).

9. Aracely de Rocchietti, "Women and the People of God," in *Through Her Eyes: Women's Theology from Latin America*, ed. Elsa Tamez (Eugene, OR: Wipf & Stock, 1989), 104.

Chapter 6 Empowerment > Coercion

1. For an important discussion of power and globalization, see Stanley Hauerwas and Samuel Wells, eds., *The Blackwell Companion to Christian Ethics* (Malden, MA: Blackwell, 2006).

2. Andy Crouch, *Playing God: Redeeming the Gift of Power* (Downers Grove, IL: InterVarsity, 2013), 37.

3. You will see other examples in the Bible where women make requests that men often do not: 2 Sam. 14:1–21; 20:16–22; 1 Kings 1:11–21; 2:13–21; Luke 18:2–5.

4. Audre Lorde, *The Master's Tools Will Never Dismantle the Master's House* (New York: Penguin, 2018), 16.

5. Kristy Garza Robinson, Natalia Kohn Rivera, and Noemi Vega Quinones, *Hermanas: Deepening Our Identity and Growing Our Influence* (Downers Grove, IL: InterVarsity, 2019), 189.

6. For a more robust discussion on the use of power in the context of American culture and politics, see James Davison Hunter, *To Change the World: The Irony, Tragedy, and Possibilities of Christianity in the Late Modern World* (Oxford: Oxford University Press, 2010), 97–193.

7. Kat Armas, *Abuelita Faith: What Women on the Margins Teach Us about Wisdom, Persistence, and Strength* (Grand Rapids: Brazos, 2021), 77.

Chapter 7 Forgiveness > Resentment

1. Howard Zehr, "Restoring Justice," in *God and the Victim: Theological Reflections on Evil, Victimization, Justice, and Forgiveness*, ed. Lisa Barnes Lampman (Grand Rapids: Eerdmans, 1999), loc. 1721–23, Kindle.

2. Tiffany Bluhm, *Prey Tell: Why We Silence Women Who Tell the Truth and How Everyone Can Speak Up* (Grand Rapids: Brazos, 2021), 81.

3. See Joseph B. Lumpkin, *The Negro Bible—the Slave Bible: Select Parts of the Holy Bible for the Use of the Negro Slaves in the British West-India Islands* (Blountsville, AL: Fifth Estate, 2019).

4. For more on racial trauma, see Sheila Wise Rowe, *Healing Racial Trauma: The Road to Resilience* (Downers Grove, IL: InterVarsity, 2020), 141.

5. For more on generational trauma, see Jacqueline T. Dyer, "From Historical Trauma to Shalom," in *Gospel Haymanot: A Constructive Theology and Critical Reflection of African and Diasporic Christianity*, ed. Vince L. Bantu (Chicago: Urban Ministries, 2020).

6. Reconciliation is about bringing people back into right relationship. Brenda Salter McNeil writes in *Roadmap to Reconciliation 2.0* that "in order for reconciliation to occur, there must be repentance, justice and forgiveness" (25). This chapter is dedicated to one component that is necessary for reconciliation to occur but will not discuss how to bring people back into healthy relationships (reconciliation). If you are interested in exploring reconciliation further, see Brenda Salter McNeil, *Roadmap to Reconciliation 2.0: Moving Communities into Unity, Wholeness and Justice* (Downers Grove, IL: InterVarsity, 2020).

7. Empirical secular research has shown the psychological and physical benefits of forgiveness as a tool in the progress of healing. See Yu-Rim Lee and Robert D. Enright, "A Meta-Analysis of the Association between Forgiveness of Others and Physical Health," *Psychology & Health* 34, no. 5 (May 4, 2019): 626–43.

8. Orlando Costas, *Christ Outside the Gate: Mission Beyond Christendom* (Eugene, OR: Wipf & Stock, 2005), 23.

9. For the practical outworking of forgiveness within early Christian community, see Ched Myers and Elaine Enns, *Ambassadors of Reconciliation: New Testament Reflections on Restorative Justice and Peacemaking*, vol. 1 (Maryknoll, NY: Orbis, 2009), chap. 3.

10. N. T. Wright, *The Lord and His Prayer* (Grand Rapids: Eerdmans, 2014), 54.

11. To dive into the difficulty and nature of discerning and accepting apologies, see Elizabeth Porter, *Connecting Peace, Justice, and Reconciliation* (Boulder, CO: Lynne Rienner, 2015), chap. 6.

12. For a powerful book on finding power in the act of forgiving terrible racial violence, see Anthony B. Thompson and Denise George, *Called to Forgive: The Charleston Church Shooting: A Victim's Husband and the Path to Healing and Peace* (Minneapolis: Bethany House, 2019). For a book that helps with the practical nuts and bolts of interpersonal forgiveness and healing, see John Paul Lederach, *Reconcile: Conflict Transformation for Ordinary Christians* (Harrisonburg, VA: Herald, 2014).

13. To see how forgiveness can happen on a societal scale, see Desmond Tutu, *No Future Without Forgiveness* (New York: Random House, 2000).

Chapter 8 Rest > Grind

1. To explore the importance of Sabbath and rest in the Old Testament, see Gen. 2:2; Exod. 16:23; 20:11; Isa. 56:2–7.

2. For more on the concept of Sabbath as resistance, see Walter Brueggemann, *Sabbath as Resistance: Saying No to the Culture of Now* (Louisville: Westminster John Knox, 2014).

3. For resources to start down the path of emotional growth, see Peter Scazzero, *Emotionally Healthy Spirituality: It's Impossible to Be Spiritually Mature, While Remaining Emotionally Immature* (Grand Rapids: Zondervan, 2017); and John Mark Comer, *The Ruthless Elimination of Hurry: How to Stay Emotionally Healthy and Spiritually Alive in the Chaos of the Modern World* (Colorado Springs: WaterBrook, 2019).

Chapter 9 Cross > Sword

1. Erica Chenoweth and Maria J. Stephan, *Why Civil Resistance Works: The Strategic Logic of Nonviolent Conflict* (New York: Columbia University Press, 2012), 292.

2. Even from a Western theological perspective, the deck is stacked against Jesus! We sit within a very violent Constantinian legacy, having settled land under the violent Doctrine of Discovery. The reformers never let go of their Dark Ages violent tendencies, and dispensationalism has been used to conveniently ignore Jesus on this point.

3. Walter Wink, "The Myth of Redemptive Violence," *The Bible in Transmission*, Spring 1999, Bible Society, https://www2.goshen.edu/~joannab/women/wink99.pdf.

4. Frantz Fanon, *The Wretched of the Earth*, trans. Richard Philcox (New York: Grove, 2005), 33.

5. Those who immediately want to respond with Romans 13 as a Christian justification for violence should see Preston Sprinkle and Andrew Rillera, *Fight: A Christian Case for Nonviolence* (Colorado Springs: David C. Cook, 2013); and John Howard Yoder, *The Politics of Jesus*, 2nd ed. (Grand Rapids: Eerdmans, 1994).

6. To dive deeper into the interpretation of these verses, see Stanley Hauerwas, *Matthew: Brazos Theological Commentary on the Bible* (Grand Rapids: Brazos, 2015), 58–72; Richard Hays, *The Moral Vision of the New Testament, Community, Cross, New Creation: A Contemporary Introduction to New Testament Ethics* (San Francisco: Harper, 1996), chap. 14; and David Gushee and Glenn Stassen, *Kingdom Ethics: Following Jesus in Contemporary Context*, 2nd ed. (Grand Rapids: Eerdmans, 2017), chap. 5.

7. For more on this radical love, see Howard Thurman, *Jesus and the Disinherited* (Boston: Beacon Press, 2022), chap. 5.

8. For a discussion on how these teachings relate to other biblical teachings, including the Old Testament, see Ronald J. Sider, *If Jesus Is Lord: Loving Our Enemies in an Age of Violence* (Grand Rapids: Baker Academic, 2019), 147.

9. For a good overview on how the early church responded nonviolently, see Sprinkle and Rillera, *Fight*, chap. 8.

10. Cecil John Cadoux, *The Early Christian Attitude to War: A Contribution to the History of Christian Ethics* (London: FB&c, 2015), 204.

11. To explore the church history developments related to violence, war, nonviolence, and enemy love, see Lisa Sowle Cahill, *Blessed Are the Peacemakers: Pacifism, Just War, and Peacebuilding* (Minneapolis: Fortress, 2019).

12. Wonhee Anne Joh, *Heart of the Cross: A Postcolonial Christology* (Louisville: Westminster John Knox, 2006), 73.

13. Dennis R. Edwards, *Might from the Margins: The Gospel's Power to Turn the Tables on Injustice* (Harrisonburg, VA: Herald, 2020), 55.

14. William T. Cavanaugh, *Migrations of the Holy: God, State, and the Political Meaning of the Church* (Grand Rapids: Eerdmans, 2011), loc. 1746, Kindle.

15. For those interested in exploring how Christians are to respond to the violence of war, I suggest Robert W. Brimlow, *What About Hitler? Wrestling with Jesus's Call to Nonviolence in an Evil World* (Grand Rapids: Brazos, 2006); Stanley Hauerwas, *War and the American Difference: Theological Reflections on Violence and National Identity* (Grand Rapids: Baker Academic, 2011); and John Roth, "Choosing Against War," in *War: Four Christian Views*, ed. Robert G. Clouse (Winona Lake, IN: BMH Books, 1986).

16. Srdja Popovic and Matthew Miller, "Blueprint for Revolution," in *Why Civil Resistance Works*.

17. David C. Cramer and Myles Werntz, *A Field Guide to Christian Nonviolence: Key Thinkers, Activists, and Movements for the Gospel of Peace* (Grand Rapids: Baker Academic, 2022).

18. Serene Jones, *Trauma and Grace: Theology in a Ruptured World*, 2nd ed. (Louisville: Westminster John Knox, 2019), 81.

19. To explore how nonviolent resistance has been used in Latin America to affect change, see Philip McManus and Gerald W. Schlabach, eds., *Relentless Persistence: Nonviolent Action in Latin America* (Eugene, OR: Wipf & Stock, 2004).

20. A great example of this is an organization called Raw Tools. They take decommissioned and donated guns and turn them into gardening tools. See Raw Tools: Disarm Hearts, Forge Peace, Cultivate Justice, https://rawtools.org/.

21. To explore how the way of Jesus impacts all of life, check out this oldie but a goodie: Guy Franklin Hershberger, *The Way of the Cross in Human Relations* (Harrisonburg, VA: Herald, 2010).

22. All stats taken from "National Statistics," National Coalition Against Domestic Violence, accessed December 14, 2021, https://ncadv.org/STATISTICS.

23. For a few case studies on contemporary peacemaking, see Cahill, *Blessed Are the Peacemakers*, chap. 9.

Chapter 10 Mobilization > Isolation

1. Eusebius, *The History of the Church*, trans. G. A. Williamson, ed. Andrew Louth (London: Penguin, 1990), 7.22.

2. Rodney Stark, *The Triumph of Christianity: How the Jesus Movement Became the World's Largest Religion* (New York: HarperCollins, 2012), 118.

3. This book was written during the worldwide Covid-19 pandemic that began in 2019. How prophetic and instructive this lesson of church history is for our current cultural moment.

4. M. Shawn Copeland, *Enfleshing Freedom: Body, Race, and Being* (Minneapolis: Fortress, 2010).

5. While there has been a massive decline in church membership and attendance in many Western churches since 2000, many Pentecostal (charismatic) movements in the US are thriving and growing. It is incumbent upon the Western church to sit at the feet of the global and Pentecostal church to learn.

6. Dietrich Bonhoeffer, *Letters and Papers from Prison* (Minneapolis: Fortress, 2015), 382–83.

7. Some good books on the topic of the church and justice are Gregg Okesson, *A Public Missiology: How Local Churches Witness to a Complex World* (Grand Rapids: Baker Academic, 2020); David T. Finch, *Faithful Presence: Seven Disciplines That Shape the Church for Mission* (Downers Grove, IL: InterVarsity, 2016); Adam Gustine, *Becoming a Just Church: Cultivating Communities of God's Shalom* (Downers Grove, IL: InterVarsity, 2019); and Stephen Offut, David F. Bronkema, Krisanne Vaillancourt Murphy, Robb Davis, and Gregg Okesson, *Advocating for Justice: An Evangelical Vision for Transforming Systems and Structures* (Grand Rapids: Baker Academic, 2016), chap. 5.

8. Robert Chao Romero, *Brown Church: Five Centuries of Latina/o Social Justice, Theology, and Identity* (Downers Grove, IL: InterVarsity, 2020), 217.

Conclusion

1. Diane G. Chen, *Luke: A New Covenant Commentary* (Eugene, OR: Cascade, 2017), 71.

2. Eric Mason, *Woke Church: An Urgent Call for Christians in America to Confront Racism and Injustice* (Chicago: Moody, 2018), 48.

3. Elizabeth Conde-Frazier, S. Steve Kang, and Gary A. Parrett, *A Many-Colored Kingdom: Multicultural Dynamics for Spiritual Formation* (Grand Rapids: Baker Academic, 2004), 169.

Scripture Index

J.W. Buck is a church planter, filmmaker, teacher, and faith-based entrepreneur. With undergraduate degrees in biblical studies and ministry, J.W. has his PhD in intercultural studies, with a focus on the problem of racial violence. He is a cofounder of Pax, a Christian organization designed to inspire and equip the next generation through slow, beautiful, Jesus-centered content created by people of color. He and his wife, Sarswatie, live in Tucson, Arizona, with their three children.

Connect with J.W.

JWBuck.org

Inspire the Next Generation with Jesus-Centered Content

Pax is a faith-based nonprofit dedicated to inspiring and equipping the next generation with beautiful, Jesus-centered, slow content created by people of color.

To learn more, visit Pax online:

Pax StoryArc Publication - madeforpax.org/storyarc

Pax Church Resources - madeforpax.org/churchresources

Pax Marketplace - madeforpax.org/marketplace

MadeForPax   Pax

MadeForPax.org

Connect with
BakerBooks
Relevant. Intelligent. Engaging.

Sign up for announcements about new and upcoming titles at

BakerBooks.com/SignUp

@ReadBakerBooks